RAVANA

RAVANA

DESTINY'S CURSED

Deepam Chatterjee

AMARYLLIS

AMARYLLIS

An imprint of Manjul Publishing House Pvt. Ltd.
• C-16, Sector 3, Noida, Uttar Pradesh 201 301, India
Website: www.manjulindia.com
Registered Office:
• 2nd Floor, Usha Preet Complex, 42 Malviya Nagar,
Bhopal 462 003 – India
Distribution Centres
Ahmedabad, Bengaluru, Chennai, Hyderabad,
Kochi, Kolkata, Mumbai, Noida, Pune

Ravana: Destiny's Cursed by Deepam Chatterjee

This paperback edition first published in India in 2025

ISBN 978-93-5543-618-4

Cover design: Trinankur Banerjee

Printed and bound in India by Repro India Limited

To my parents
Manjushree and Varun

You gave me the freedom
to witness, understand and accept
the eternal Rama-Ravana battle
that goes on within.

Contents

Preface

Why write yet another book on Ravana? There are countless retellings, each recounting the rise and fall of the Asura King of Lanka, a larger-than-life figure entwined in the lore of Hindu mythology. However, *Ravana: Destiny's Cursed* brings a perspective I felt was missing from these accounts—a journey that delves into the depths of Ravana's soul, his past and future lives, and the very essence of his role in the cosmic order. This book illuminates a side of Ravana not often considered, viewing his character not just as a fearsome antagonist but as a profound, complex figure who, in his final moments, glimpses into the grand design of his existence.

The story of Ravana has intrigued me for its complexity, its contradictions, and the rich nuances often overlooked in simplistic depictions. He is, without doubt, a figure of immense villainy in Indian lore, but behind this image lies a man of vast intellect, intense devotion, and an unbridled ambition that both propelled him and became his undoing. This book arose from a desire to understand the motivations, emotions, and internal conflicts that drove Ravana. His narrative deserved more than a simplistic portrayal as a mere villain. A complex man, he embodied the contradictions of a scholar, warrior, and devout follower of Shiva plagued by arrogance and unchecked ambition.

This book takes readers to Ravana's final moments when he recounts the unravelling of his and his loyal brother Kumbhakarna's incarnations as Jaya-Vijaya, Hiranyaksha-Hiranyakashyapa, and ultimately as Shishupal and Dantavakra. In these revelations, Ravana perceives himself as part of a grand cosmic design, a being destined to oppose divine figures across lives. In his role as a counterpoint to Rama, Ravana realises his place within the narrative of good versus evil, as both an instrument of divine will and a man ensnared by his own choices.

As ambassadors of evil, one character flaw which consistently defined Ravana, Hiranyakashyapa, and Shishupal throughout their incarnations was pride. In fact, it was their unyielding arrogance that originally led Jaya and Vijaya, the celestial gatekeepers of Vaikuntha, into the cycle of three cursed births.

Pride, born from the heights of power or position, invariably leads to downfall, and the path to redemption is often an arduous, humbling one. This tale is a reminder to remain constantly vigilant against arrogance, as even a single moment of arrogance can dismantle empires built over a lifetime.

Our tale begins with Jaya and Vijaya, purported to be reincarnations of the primordial demons Madhu and Kaitabha. We first meet Jaya and Vijaya as doorkeepers of Vaikuntha, where their fateful encounter with the four Sanakadi Kumaras—ancient, childlike sages—would shape their destiny. Overcome by pride, the gatekeepers treat these revered sages with disdain. In response, the usually guileless sages adopt a saddened, grave tone, casting upon the duo a curse of immense consequence: they are to fall from heaven and enter the cycle of mortal existence.

Lord Vishnu himself intervenes, offering Jaya and Vijaya a choice: they can be born as his ardent devotees for seven lifetimes or as his fierce adversaries for three. Desperate to minimise their time apart from their Lord, Jaya and Vijaya choose the latter. All seems forgiven as the Kumaras rejoice upon meeting Vishnu, yet the curse must unfold. And so, Jaya and Vijaya soon vanish from Vaikuntha, only to be reborn in the womb of Diti, where their destiny as Hiranyakashyapa and Hiranyaksha begins. Thus commences the Daityas' terrible reign on earth, setting into motion the cycle of their ultimate redemption, as Vishnu descends into the mortal realms, assuming *four* separate avatars to liberate his beloved gatekeepers from their three cursed incarnations.

While most accounts portray Ravana as a tyrant, he was also an individual of great intellectual and spiritual depth. His profound knowledge of the Vedas, mastery of the sacred scriptures, and expertise in various arts reflected an insatiable thirst for understanding. Beyond his reputation for wrath, Ravana's musical skills with the *Rudra Veena* were celebrated, and the grandeur of Lanka itself shone as a testament to his architectural vision and creativity. His devotion to Lord Shiva was unwavering, and he earned divine blessings through rigorous penance, a spiritual discipline that revealed both the intensity of his dedication and the dangers of his pride.

This side of Ravana—the scholar and the devotee—adds layers to his character. Here was a seeker, a man striving for enlightenment, yet perpetually hindered by his own pride and ambition. His reverence for Shiva, led to him composing the powerful *Shiva Tandava Stotram* which reflects his intense spiritual quest. However, even this journey was marred by hubris. His intellect, his skills, and his devotion were undeniable, yet they could not shield him from the temptations of power and dominance.

In portraying Ravana's story, I felt it crucial to examine his complexity and humanity. Although a mighty king and formidable adversary, Ravana was, above all, a deeply flawed man. He was weighed down by his own ego, greed, and boundless ambition, and his life was often ruled by arrogance and desire. His relationships reveal a man haunted by inner conflicts and personal strife—a man whose pride and unyielding will made him lonely, isolated even from those who cared for him the most. His bond with Mandodari, his wife, was marked by her loyalty and wisdom, qualities that could have balanced his unbridled ambition had he allowed her counsel to reach him. Mandodari's love and patience reveal Ravana's capacity for gentler emotions, but her wisdom was often silenced by his need for validation and dominance. With Kumbhakarna, his loyal brother, Ravana shared a kinship rooted in devotion, and yet Kumbhakarna's unwavering support became both a blessing and a tragedy, as he joined Ravana's misguided cause out of loyalty rather than conviction.

The contrasting wisdom of his other brother, Vibhishana, challenged Ravana, forcing him to confront the moral path he persistently chose to ignore.

Vibhishana's counsel represented the voice of reason, one that Ravana dismissed to his detriment, emphasising his tragic inability to yield even to the guidance of those who loved him.

His sister Minakshi (Shurpanakha), ignited his vengeful side. Her humiliation and disfigurement at the hands of Lakshmana stirred his anger, and yet, beneath his fury was a deep sorrow and self-doubt over his failure to protect her. Even his strained relationship with his son Meghnada (Indrajit), reflects his complexity. Ravana was a proud father yet, tragically, one whose ambitions eventually endangered all those he cherished. Meghnada's prowess and loyalty filled Ravana with pride, but he failed to temper his son's blinding arrogance, and the risks Meghnada's actions posed to his own bloodline.

These strained bonds, marked by both love and torment, reveal a Ravana torn between his heart and his aspirations. None could truly breach the walls of his pride. His genius as a scholar, his passion for the arts, his remarkable wisdom, and even his love for Shiva were ultimately darkened by the shadows he cast upon himself. He was a man who loved but was ultimately isolated by his unyielding ego, and who, in fighting others, was in fact wrestling with himself.

Ravana's relentless ambition became both his driving force and his undoing. His conquest of Lanka, his seizing of the *Pushpaka Vimana* from his half-brother Kubera, and his forceful abduction of countless women, highlight his unquenchable thirst for dominance, thereby incurring the rage of the gods and earning divine wrath.

Ravana's story is punctuated by multiple curses,

from Narada's foretelling of his tragic fate, to Shiva's punishment of trapping him under His great mountain abode Kailash, echoing the impending consequences of his fatal flaw. The more he amassed power, the more he alienated himself, isolating him within a fortress of ego from which he could not escape. His arrogance invited ruin, not only upon himself but upon all he held dear: the fates of Kumbhakarna, Mandodari, Meghnada, and eventually Lanka itself, were sealed.

And yet, there is a certain nobility in his suffering. As he faces his end, Ravana speaks to the mortal reader, his voice reverberating across ages, warning against the very flaws that led to his doom—hubris, unchecked desire, indulgence in worldly pleasures.

The legend of Ravana, I believe, still resonates deeply, with lessons for modern sensibilities. His message is both cautionary and universal, a testament to the perils of human frailties that transcend time. In our exploration of his triumphs, his wisdom, and his fall from grace, we can recognise parts of ourselves. Through this book, I hope to share a narrative that transcends his villainy to explore the nuances of his character—a man marked not only by his darkness but also by his intense passions, his deep devotion, and his isolation in a world that both revered and feared him.

This tale of unchecked ambition speaks across time, warning of the dangers inherent in the unrestrained pursuit of power. In an oft-repeated soliloquy, Ravana might have cautioned today's mortals: '*Ambition consumed my soul; beware its allure. Hubris and worldly pleasures imperil the spirit, and what begins as strength may end in ruin.*'

At its heart, the book is more than an exploration of a mythological figure; it is a study of the human condition and morality. Through Ravana's struggle, we encounter reflections on ambition's double edge, the tenuous boundary between devotion and obsession, and the tragic isolation that often accompanies unbridled ego. Ravana's final vision—a revelation of past and future lives—serves as a reminder of the cyclical nature of existence, where actions ripple through time and consequences are inescapable.

Ravana's story challenges us to see beyond simplistic notions of good and evil, inviting empathy for a character as flawed and vulnerable as he was powerful. As readers journey through his heart and mind, they are encouraged to reflect on their own lives, to confront the allure of ambition, and to recognise the potential pitfalls of unchecked emotions and uncontrolled impulses. In Ravana's story, we may find a mirror for our own lives, reflecting both the strength and the flaws that make us human.

Ravana: Destiny's Cursed was born from a desire to tell Ravana's tale not as a myth, but as a story of humanity, with all its sorrow, struggle, and inevitable consequences. It is a journey that, while unique, invites every reader to find echoes of their own journey within it. It is a journey into Ravana's heart—a profound and timeless exploration where his vulnerabilities, humanity, and destiny converge. Here, the boundaries of time and morality blur, and we are reminded that the dance between light and shadow is an eternal one.

Prologue

Beginning of the End

The sea roared with fury, its waves crashing against the shore of Lanka as though the ocean itself sought to devour the island. Dark, swirling clouds churned above, casting the battlefield in a shadowy half-light, their ominous shapes mirrored in the churning waters below. The earth trembled, cracked open by the weight of battle, and a suffocating air of doom hung heavy over the scene, a palpable reminder of the fate that was to unfold. The skies had become a battlefield of their own, as though the gods themselves were warring above. Lightning split the heavens, jagged streaks of light tearing through the darkness, illuminating the chaos below in brief flashes.

On one side of the battlefield, seated atop the mighty shoulders of Hanuman, was Rama. His presence was serene, though the flames of war surrounded him. His face was calm, eyes fixed ahead, yet his body was a taut instrument of purpose, a divine figure of unwavering resolve. The massive figure of Hanuman, towering above the soldiers and beasts alike, moved with swift precision, his movements defying the burden of the prince he bore.

Across the field, in a flying chariot drawn by demonic asses, floated Ravana. His dark silhouette hovered like a malevolent spectre over the battlefield, the wheels of his chariot spinning with the power of ancient magic, the wind howling around him. The air itself seemed to twist and warp in his presence, the very fabric of reality bending to his will. Ravana's black robes billowed behind him, his armour gleaming under the faint light of the storm-laden sky. His eyes burned with the fire of a thousand lifetimes of hatred, ambition, and pride.

In the distance, the war raged on—Vanaras clashing with Rakshasas, steel meeting flesh, the screams of the dying swallowed by the thunderous roar of the heavens. Yet, for all the violence around them, it was as though the world itself had become silent, waiting for the clash of two titanic forces destined to meet.

Ravana watched Rama with a cold, calculating gaze. He had fought countless battles, but none had felt as weighted with inevitability as this one. He knew the prince was no ordinary man; he knew the truth, even if the world did not yet understand. This was not a simple battle between a demon king and a prince in exile—this was the culmination of forces far greater than either of them. Rama was Vishnu, incarnated in mortal form, who had come to end Ravana's reign.

And yet, Ravana was undeterred.

He stood tall in his chariot, his form flickering and twisting as he disappeared from view, only to reappear in a different location. The battlefield was his domain, and in this moment, he was a shadow among shadows, moving unseen, a master of illusion. One moment, he was before Rama, taunting him with his proximity, and the next, he had vanished into thin air, only to strike from another angle. Each time, he unleashed a volley of arrows—arrows dark as night—their tips glowing with the malice of a thousand curses.

But Rama was not easily deceived. His divine eyes tracked Ravana's every movement, his arrows flying with precision, cutting through the illusions with the ease of a master archer. His movements, though restrained, held the grace of the divine, each arrow an extension of his will, each strike a testament to his righteousness. Seated atop Hanuman's broad shoulders, Rama appeared untouchable, a god among men, his bow strung and ready for the next strike.

Ravana roared in fury, frustrated by Rama's calm, unshaken demeanour. He would not be defeated so easily. With a gesture, he summoned the full might of his sorcery, casting his hand toward the sky. The clouds above seemed to tear open, and from the darkness descended a horde of grotesque, illusory creatures—demons with fiery eyes and wings that blotted out the sun, their screeches tearing through the air as they descended upon Rama.

Yet, even amidst this chaotic storm, Rama did not falter. His arrows flew like lightning, cutting down the illusions as they came, each shaft carrying with it the weight of dharma itself. Hanuman, beneath him, swatted away the creatures with his mighty fists, his strength matching and easily surpassing the shadows conjured by Ravana's magic.

Undeterred, Ravana's chariot soared higher, a dark shape against the roiling clouds. His hands moved swiftly, summoning one final illusion—a mirror image of himself. Across the battlefield, a second Ravana appeared, just as powerful, just as menacing, as if mocking the very notion of death. The illusion moved with the same force and malice as Ravana himself, unleashing a rain of arrows from above, turning the sky black with their number.

For a moment, it seemed as though the heavens themselves would fall under the weight of Ravana's attack. But Rama's arrows sang in response, a divine melody cutting through the thundering rain, each shot finding its mark, each illusion shattering into nothingness. The skies parted as the power of Vishnu flowed through his mortal hands.

The earth beneath them trembled again, fissures spreading across the ground as though the planet itself quaked in anticipation of what was to come. The sea crashed violently against the shores, waves rising like mountains only to fall again with devastating force. The elements seemed to recognise the significance of this moment, the air thick with the scent of inevitability.

High above, in his chariot, Ravana's breath came fast and hard. His power, though formidable, was waning. He could feel it—deep in his bones, in the marrow of his soul—the inexorable pull of fate. His entire life had been a march toward this moment, though he had fought it every step of the way. He had battled gods, conquered worlds, and bent the universe to his will. And yet, here he was, facing the end, knowing that it had been written in the stars long before his birth.

His eyes found Vibhishana, standing at a distance on the battlefield, watching with a sorrowful gaze. Ravana's heart twisted with the sting of betrayal, yet he understood. He had always understood, even as he despised it. Vibhishana, his own brother, had chosen the righteous path, forsaking his own blood to stand with Rama. He preferred the human way of life to the Rakshasa code. He had always dreamt of becoming human. He abhorred the asuric life. The betrayal was deep, but it was also inevitable.

And now, as Ravana's gaze locked with his brother's, understanding dawned. Vibhishana had revealed the secret of his death to Rama. The navel—his life force—was the key. Vibhishana had always been destined to reveal the secret to Ravana's end.

Ravana's lips curled into a bitter smile. Of course, it would come to this. Vibhishana, the one who had chosen betrayal, had sealed his fate. Yet there was no hatred left in him, only the cold acceptance of a truth he had long known but refused to confront.

As if on cue, Rama drew his final arrow, the *Brahmastra.* Its tip glowed with the fire of a thousand suns, its energy humming with the power of the universe itself. The arrow was divine—unstoppable, unbreakable. Ravana could feel the weight of its presence even from a distance. This was the arrow that would end him. This was the culmination of his defiance, his ambition, his pride.

He glanced at the battlefield below. The bodies of his soldiers were scattered like broken toys, the land of Lanka, his kingdom, torn asunder by war. The sea raged around him, the wind howling in his ears. And yet, amidst the destruction, he felt a strange peace. This, after all, was his role in the grand design.

Rama released the arrow.

It flew straight and true, a streak of divine light cutting through the sky, cutting through the illusions, cutting through time itself. Ravana, still in his chariot, felt the force of the *Brahmastra* as it pierced his navel. Pain surged through him, but it was not the physical agony that struck him hardest—it was the knowledge that this was not the end. He had to live out another lifetime in the coming *Dwapara yuga*.

'Next time, make it quick. Don't give me a long life like this one. Finish it fast.' He whispered to the firmament.

He staggered, his body convulsing as his chariot wavered and fell toward the ground. The world blurred around him, the sounds of the battlefield fading into a dull hum. As he crumpled to the earth, his vision darkening, Ravana's mind raced.

'I am Ravana,' he whispered, his voice barely audible amidst the storm, 'and without me, your gods would be nothing. Without killing me, O Rama, you wouldn't become the man who shall be worshipped as God for all eternity.'

His lips curled into a smile, a smile that carried the weight of lifetimes, of victories and defeats, of ambition and ruin. He had played his part. Without his defiance, without his fall, there could be no rise for the gods. Without darkness, there could be no light.

And with that, the great king of Lanka, the terror of gods and men alike, fell.

And, as Ravana fell, his many lives began to flash in front of his eyes...

'Ah, mortals and gods who witness my fall, gather and listen to the words of Ravana, the mighty king of Lanka, as I lay here on this battlefield, life ebbing away. My existence, a saga of unparalleled might and grievous folly, is a lesson written in the ink of blood and ambition, a cautionary tale for all who seek power beyond their grasp.

'I was born to conquer, to rule, to shape the world according to my vision. My intellect rivalled the greatest of sages, my mastery of the Vedas unmatched. My strength shook the heavens. I performed penances that earned me boons from the gods themselves. Yet, despite my might and wisdom, I was undone by my own hubris. In my defiance, I sought to challenge the divine, to bend the cosmic order to my will.

'In my arrogance, I seized Sita, not out of love, but to defy the gods. Blinded by pride, I did not foresee the ruin it would bring upon me and my kin. My sons, my brothers, my loyal warriors—all fell because of my folly. Indrajit, my mightiest son, invincible in battle, brought low by the machinations of fate. Kumbhakarna, my indomitable brother, a titan among men, struck down despite his valiant heart. Their deaths weigh heavily upon me, their blood a testament to my own failings and the inevitable doom of hubris.

'And Vibhishana, my own blood, turned traitor. Your betrayal is a wound deeper than any weapon, a rift that cleaves the heart and soul. You, who once stood by my side, now revel in my downfall. Yet, it is a betrayal I must accept, a part of the karmic wheel that turns inexorably, binding us all in its relentless cycle.'

—Ravana, Emperor of Lanka

ONE

Madhu and Kaitabha

Darkness and Activity

In the mystical realm of creation, deep in the tranquil waters of the cosmic ocean, Lord Vishnu lay in his eternal *Yoga Nidra*—a divine slumber, preserving the universe in perfect stillness. From this stillness, two malevolent beings were born: Madhu and Kaitabha. These asuras emerged from the wax in Vishnu's ears, their forms nurtured by the dark attributes of *tamas* and *rajas*, the two primal forces that govern creation and destruction.

Above them, from the navel of Vishnu, a lotus bloomed, and upon this lotus sat Brahma, the creator. He remained focused on the work of crafting a new universe from the remnants of the old one. But Madhu and Kaitabha, filled with demonic energy, grew restless. Their power swelled, and with it, their arrogance. The chaos within them could not be contained.

For many ages, they thrived, consuming the essence of the waters in which Vishnu lay, drawing nourishment from the very ocean of existence. In their arrogance, they believed themselves invincible. However, they were soon drawn to the echoing vibrations of a primordial mantra, calling them toward deeper contemplation. For a thousand years, they meditated, absorbed in devotion to the cosmic force. The power of their penance was so great that it summoned Mother Mahamaya, the primaeval Goddess, who governs the illusion that binds the world.

Appearing before them in a blaze of divine light, Mahamaya addressed them with benevolence. 'Your devotion is praiseworthy,' she said. 'Ask for a boon, and it shall be granted.'

Madhu and Kaitabha, lost in their delusions of grandeur, requested, 'Grant us the power to choose the moment of our death. Let it not be determined by fate, but by our will.'

Mahamaya, with her ever-knowing smile, granted their request. 'So be it,' she proclaimed. 'Your lives will now endure until you choose to relinquish them. No one in the heavens or the underworld can defeat you, unless you yourself desire it.'

Empowered by this boon, the asuras became virtually invincible. But, as with many beings blessed with great power, they soon turned toward darkness. They ravaged the worlds, spreading chaos and destruction, their egos swelling with each conquest. No celestial force could stand against them, and they revelled in the ruin left in their wake.

Their gaze soon fell upon Brahma, seated atop his lotus, creating new worlds and beings. Enraged by his lofty position, Madhu and Kaitabha confronted him, their eyes gleaming with malevolence. 'Old man!' they taunted. 'You sit so high, as if you are worthy of such honour. Descend from your throne, for it is we, the mighty, who deserve to sit where you are. Or, if you refuse, prove your worth by fighting us!'

Brahma, knowing that he could not defeat the asuras, felt a wave of dread wash over him. The boon granted by Mahamaya had made them immune to the power of any deity, and he realised that only Vishnu could save him now. Without hesitation, Brahma fled from the demons, seeking refuge at Vishnu's feet.

But Vishnu, still in his *Yoga Nidra*, remained unmoved by Brahma's pleas. The creator, his heart filled with desperation, prayed fervently to Devi Mahamaya. 'O Mother of the universe, awaken the Preserver! Only he can vanquish these demons.'

Moved by Brahma's prayers, Mahamaya gently withdrew her veil of illusion from Vishnu's eyes. Slowly, the Lord of Preservation stirred, his gaze serene and untroubled, as if he already knew the outcome of the events to come.

Madhu and Kaitabha, relishing their perceived victory over Brahma, made their way through the cosmic ocean towards the very source of creation. 'Why seek refuge in the abode of the Preserver?' they taunted, their laughter reverberating through the waters. 'Why do you protect Brahma?' they sneered. 'Stand aside, or face our wrath.'

Vishnu, fully awake and aware of the threat, merely smiled. His calm demeanour infuriated the demons. He said, 'If you believe yourselves to be so powerful, then fight.'

Madhu and Kaitabha, blinded by their pride, accepted the challenge. They lunged at Vishnu with all their might, and thus began an epic battle, one that would last for five thousand years. The demons fought relentlessly, one after the other, their strength unyielding.

Vishnu, despite his divine might, found himself unable to defeat the asuras. They were, after all, protected by the boon that made them invulnerable to any attack unless they willed their own death. As the battle dragged on, Vishnu knew he needed more than sheer force to win. And so, through his divine mind, he called out once more to Mahamaya.

'Goddess,' he prayed, 'you granted them their strength. Help me now to turn their boon against them.'

Hearing his call, Mahamaya responded with a subtle shift in the air. 'O Vishnu,' she whispered in his mind, 'use their pride against them. Their arrogance will be their downfall. Deceive them with words, and they shall meet their end.'

Armed with this knowledge, Vishnu continued the battle, biding his time. Eventually, the asuras, growing weary from the prolonged fight, offered a brief respite.

'Let us rest,' they said. 'You, too, must be tired. It is only honourable to give each other a chance to recover.'

Vishnu agreed, and during the lull, he began to praise the asuras' strength and valour. 'I have fought many battles,' he said, 'but never have I encountered warriors as powerful as you. Your might is unparalleled. In honour of your bravery, I offer you a boon. Ask, and I shall grant it.'

The asuras, their egos swollen with pride, laughed. 'We are the victors here!' they said. 'It is not for the defeated to grant boons, but for the victors. We are the ones who should offer you a boon!'

Vishnu, feigning humility, nodded. 'Very well,' he said. 'If you are truly victorious, then grant me this one wish: that you allow me to end your lives.'

For a moment, Madhu and Kaitabha hesitated, realising too late the trap they had fallen into. But their arrogance had already sealed their fate. Bound by their own words, they reluctantly agreed. 'So be it,' they said.

With their consent, Vishnu summoned his *Sudarshan Chakra*, the divine discus, and with one swift motion, he beheaded the demons, ending their reign of terror.

The bodies of Madhu and Kaitabha fell into the cosmic ocean, their immense forms dissolving into the waters. Order was restored, and the cycle of creation continued. Brahma returned to his lotus, resuming his work, while Vishnu once again lay down to rest, the cosmos preserved by his eternal vigilance.

Thus, the two asuras who had once sought to conquer the heavens met their end, undone not by force, but by the very boon they had so arrogantly sought. Their tale would echo through the ages, a reminder of the dangers of unchecked pride and the eternal balance maintained by the cosmic forces of creation and destruction.

Madhu and Kaitabha would make a comeback in another form. Reborn as Jaya and Vijaya, they would become the gatekeepers of Vaikuntha, destined to face Vishnu again in the cycles of time to come.

Thus begins my tale.

'Mortals, learn from my tale. Power, when wielded without wisdom, leads to ruin. Know this, those who listen: before I was Ravana, I was Hiranyakashyapa, the asura king whose defiance of Vishnu led to my demise at the hands of Narasimha. And before that, in the beginning, I was Jaya, and my brother was Vijaya. We were the proud gatekeepers of Vaikuntha, the divine abode of Lord Vishnu. Our station was one of honour and power, entrusted with guarding the celestial gates against all intrusions. Our vigilance was unmatched, our devotion unquestioned. Yet, it was our pride, that insidious flaw, that proved to be our undoing.

'One day, the four Sanatkumaras, ancient sages of immense wisdom, approached the gates of Vaikuntha. Though they appear as mere children, their souls are ageless, their knowledge boundless. Puffed up with a sense of importance, we refused entry to the saints in spite of repeated entreaties. Eventually enraged, they cursed us to roam the earth as mere mortals.

'Desperate, we requested Lord Vishnu to lift the curse. The Lord gave us two options. We could either go through seven earthly lifetimes as His devotees or, three lifetimes as His arch enemies. Thereafter we could return to Vaikuntha. Without a moment's thought, we chose to become our Lord Vishnu's enemies on earth.

'In each incarnation, I challenged the divine and met my end. Yet, I am fated to be born once more as Shishupal, to meet my demise at the hands of Krishna in the Dwapara Yuga. This destiny I cannot escape. Each birth and death is a step toward the ultimate understanding, yet also a prolongation of my torment.

'The cosmos is vast, its order intricate and just. Our fall from

Vaikuntha is a testament to the dangers of pride, a reminder that true service to the divine requires humility and respect, not the arrogance of power. Heed this warning: even the mightiest can fall. In our defiance, we became the architects of our own doom.'

–Ravana, Emperor of Lanka

TWO

Jaya and Vijaya

Curse of the Manasaputras

The realms of Vaikuntha lay beyond the mortal comprehension of time and space. Here, in the dwelling of Lord Vishnu, all things were eternally serene, boundless, and bathed in the gentle light of an everlasting dawn. The lotus blooms on the celestial waters radiated a soft glow, their delicate fragrance filling the air, while the harmonious murmur of flowing streams echoed through the heavens. Nothing stirred in this realm of divine tranquillity unless willed by the Lord himself.

At the gates to the inner sanctum of Vaikuntha, where the Lord rested in serene repose upon the coils of the great serpent Ananta, stood Jaya and Vijaya, his steadfast gatekeepers. For countless aeons, they had stood guard at the threshold of Vishnu's abode, vigilant and ever-watchful, their devotion and duty to him unwavering. None could pass through these gates without their permission, and few would dare to challenge their authority.

On this day, however, as the celestial winds stirred softly through the sacred realm, the peace of Vaikuntha was to be disrupted by an event that would change the fate of the universe.

Approaching the gates were four luminous figures—the Four Kumaras, the mind-born sons of Brahma. The Ancient One, Sanaka; the Eternal One, Sanatana; the Ever-joyful One, Sanandana; and the Ever-young One, Sanatkumara. Clad in the simplest of garments, their youthful forms belied the immense wisdom they carried within. They had journeyed far, their only desire to seek an audience with the Supreme Lord, to speak with him on matters that transcended the mortal world.

As they neared the gates, their serene expressions and effortless grace should have been enough to dispel any doubts about their divine status. Yet, as Jaya and Vijaya beheld the approaching sages, they hesitated. The Kumaras, with their childlike forms, seemed to the gatekeepers to be nothing more than children, their soft features unsuited to the gravitas of Vaikuntha.

Jaya, his posture stiffening, raised his hand to halt the Kumaras in their path. 'Who are you, children?' he asked, his voice firm but not harsh. 'This is Vaikuntha, the realm of Lord Vishnu. Only the worthiest may pass through these gates.'

Sanaka, the eldest of the Kumaras, stepped forward with the calm dignity that only ancient wisdom could provide. His eyes, though youthful, held the weight of endless time. 'We are the sons of Brahma,' he said in a voice that was soft yet carried across the space between them. 'We seek an audience with Lord Vishnu.'

However, Vijaya, standing tall beside his brother, was unmoved. His devotion to Vishnu ran deep, but with it had grown a possessiveness—an overzealous sense of duty. 'The Lord rests,' Vijaya declared. 'None may disturb him.'

The Kumaras exchanged a glance, their faces still calm, untroubled by the refusal. They had encountered many who failed to see beyond surface appearances, and in their hearts, they harboured no anger or pride. They understood the gatekeepers' devotion, but it was precisely this excessive pride in their duty that troubled them.

Sanatana, the Eternal One, spoke next, his voice like the murmur of a distant stream. 'We come not to disturb, but to offer our reverence and to speak with him on matters of great importance.'

But Jaya shook his head, his resolve firm. 'It is not a time for visitors. You cannot pass.'

Sanandana, the Ever-joyful, smiled gently, his face still radiant with the peace that dwelled within him. 'Do not let our youthful forms deceive you,' he said softly. 'We are as old as creation itself. The Lord knows us, and we have come to him as seekers, not as disturbers of his peace.'

Despite the gentle words of the Kumaras, Jaya and Vijaya remained unyielding. Their devotion, though pure, had clouded their judgement, and in their hearts, a seed of pride had begun to grow—pride that they alone were worthy to stand at the gate of Vishnu.

It was then that a shift occurred, subtle but profound. The air grew heavier, and a quiet descended upon Vaikuntha, as though the very realm itself held its breath. The Kumaras, though ever serene, could sense the weight of the moment. They felt no anger, but there was sorrow in their hearts for what had to come next.

Sanatkumara, the youngest, but no less wise, stepped forward now, his voice soft but filled with the authority of one who spoke the truth. 'Your pride has blinded you,' he said, his words devoid of malice but heavy with meaning. 'You have allowed your sense of duty to overshadow your respect for those who seek the Lord's presence.'

And with that, Sanaka, the eldest, looked upon Jaya and Vijaya with compassion, though his heart was heavy. 'For your transgression, you must face the consequences,' he said, his voice as steady as the flow of time. 'We curse you, gatekeepers of Vaikuntha, to be separated from your Lord. You will be cast down to the mortal realm, far from the divine presence you so fiercely guard. Only after countless lives of suffering and separation will you come to understand the pain of being kept from the one you love.'

The words fell like a shadow upon the gatekeepers. Jaya and Vijaya, who had stood so proudly at the gates of Vaikuntha, felt the weight of the curse settle upon them like chains. They had acted not out of malice, but out of an overzealousness that had led them to disrespect the very sages they should have honoured.

It was then that the great doors to Vishnu's sanctum opened, and the Lord himself appeared. His form was radiant, a vision of calm and compassion. He had heard all that had transpired and knew that the curse, once uttered, could not be undone. Yet, he was the embodiment of mercy, and his heart ached for his beloved gatekeepers.

With a gentle smile, Vishnu greeted the Kumaras with deep respect. 'Welcome, O great sages,' he said, his voice soft and kind, 'I apologise for the transgressions of my two doorkeepers. I see the truth in your words, and I accept the justice of your curse. They must realise the folly in their actions. But I ask of you, if it is within your grace, to allow me to modify the terms of their punishment.'

The Kumaras, who bore no ill will, looked upon Vishnu with reverence. Their cursing was simply a lesson, a way to guide them back to humility and understanding. Sanaka, ever serene, nodded graciously. 'Lord Vishnu, you are the embodiment of compassion. If you wish to modify their fate, we will not stand in the way. The justice we have spoken of need not be cruel.'

Vishnu bowed his head slightly in gratitude and turned to Jaya and Vijaya, who stood with their heads bowed in shame. 'You have been cursed,' Vishnu said, his voice gentle but firm, 'and though the curse must be fulfilled, I offer you a choice. You may live seven lifetimes as my devotees, far from Vaikuntha, but ever loyal to me. Or, you may live three lifetimes as my enemies, where you will rise to great power but fall each time by my hand. The choice is yours.'

Jaya and Vijaya, their hearts heavy with the weight of their actions, looked at one another. To be separated from their Lord for seven lifetimes, even as his devotees, was unbearable. They could not fathom such a long exile from the presence they so cherished.

After a moment of silent contemplation, Jaya spoke, his voice filled with sorrowful resolve. 'We choose to live three lifetimes as your enemies, my Lord. Better to face you in battle and be defeated by your hand than to be separated from you for so long.'

Vishnu, though saddened by their fate, understood their choice. 'So be it,' he said softly. 'In each life, you will rise to great power, and in each life, you will be slain by me. Only then will you return to Vaikuntha.'

With those words, the curse took hold. Jaya and Vijaya, once the proud gatekeepers of Vaikuntha, were cast down to the earthly realm, their divine forms dissolving into the fabric of the universe. Yet, even as they fell, they held fast to the one truth that gave them comfort: they would return to their Lord, no matter how long their mortal journey took.

The Kumaras bowed respectfully to Vishnu, their faces calm and serene, and followed him into the celestial halls of Vaikuntha.

And so, with the curse and the blessing spoken, the inevitable began to unfold. Jaya and Vijaya, the once-proud gatekeepers of Vaikuntha, were cast down from the heavens, their forms dissolving into the world of mortals. The skies of Vaikuntha wept, and even the lotuses in the eternal waters bowed their heads in sorrow.

Their fall from Vaikuntha would echo through the ages, entwining with the destinies of gods and mortals alike, and though the path ahead was fraught with darkness and separation, they knew that in the end, all roads would lead back to their beloved Lord.

THREE

The Hiranyas

Inauspicious Origins

As the sun sank beneath the horizon, the world stood on the brink of a twilight that seemed deeper than usual. The heavens were ablaze with hues of crimson and violet, but there was an unsettling stillness in the air—a silence that marked the transition between light and dark, life and death. It was a time governed by ominous forces, when demons and spirits stirred and shadows lengthened over the earth.

But Diti, the daughter of Prajapati Daksha, paid little heed to such portents. She stood at the entrance of her dwelling, her gaze fixed on the dimming horizon, her heart stirred by a yearning she could no longer contain. Her body was alive with desire, an inexplicable urgency surging through her veins.

Inside the ashram, her husband, Maharishi Kashyapa, was still lost in his deep meditation. But Diti's patience had long since worn thin. A fierce hunger gnawed at her, an insistent call that overpowered reason and caution. She had waited too long. Now, she could wait no more.

Diti knew well that this hour—this twilight—belonged to the Rakshasas, the ghosts, the demons of the world.

She knew the risk that came with yielding to her desires at such a time. But the knowledge could not suppress the flame that had ignited within her. Her mind was filled with one thought, and one thought only: to conceive. To bear children of might and power.

The ashram's grounds were quiet, yet the stillness held an unsettling quality. As the last traces of sunlight vanished, a strange chill crept into the air. Diti felt it, but her desire overpowered any sense of foreboding.

At long last, Kashyapa stirred from his meditation. His presence, serene and luminous, filled the space as he stepped toward Diti, his eyes reflecting the fading light of the sun. He could sense the tension within her, the urgent energy that clung to her like a second skin. He saw, too, the recklessness that had seized her heart.

'Dearest Diti,' Kashyapa began, his voice calm but touched with concern, 'your heart is restless. What troubles you?'

Her gaze met his, and her eyes burned with a fierce, unrelenting need. 'Lord, I cannot wait any longer,' she said, her voice trembling with the force of her emotions. 'The desire for children consumes me. I feel it like fire in my veins. I beg you—let us unite.'

Kashyapa's eyes darkened, and a deep frown creased his brow. The weight of her request hung heavily in the air. He could feel the unnatural stillness around them, the twilight thick with the presence of dark, unseen forces. His wisdom told him what she refused to see.

'Beloved,' he began, his voice calm but edged with warning, 'this hour belongs not to the gods, but to the demons. The forces that rule this time are dark and inauspicious. If we act now, our children will be touched by this darkness. Do you not understand the consequences?'

But Diti's desire had taken hold of her completely. Her mind was ablaze with a single thought: to create life. 'I care not for omens or portents,' she replied, her voice sharp with impatience. 'I have waited long enough. I want children, O Kashyapa. Sons who will be powerful, who will shape the world.'

Kashyapa's frown deepened. He understood the gravity of what she asked. His foresight, clear as the light of the stars, told him of the chaos her desire would unleash. 'Diti,' he said softly, 'if you insist on this, know that the children you bear will be no ordinary offspring. They will be demons, beings of great power and terrible consequence. Their reign will bring suffering to the world.'

But Diti, her pride ignited, met his gaze with fierce resolve. 'Then let them be demons!' she declared. 'Let them be the most powerful beings to ever walk the earth. I am not afraid. I will bear them proudly.'

Kashyapa looked at her long and hard, the weight of his knowledge pressing down upon him. He could see that her will was immovable, her desires unchecked. To deny her now would only deepen her frustration and push her further into defiance.

With a sigh of resignation, he nodded. 'Very well, Diti,' he said. 'But know this—what we do tonight is against the natural order. The children you bear will bring calamity.'

And so, despite the inauspicious hour, despite his

wisdom and the warnings that tugged at his mind, Kashyapa yielded to Diti's insistent plea.

The act was done. The night grew darker, and the stars blinked into existence overhead as the act of creation was completed. But there was no peace in the air, no serenity in the stillness that followed. Diti lay beside her husband, a fierce sense of satisfaction blooming within her. Her body felt heavy with the promise of life, and her heart swelled with pride. Kashyapa's words, laden with caution, weighed little in her mind. She had got what she wanted—she would bear sons of great power. The future, whatever it held, did not concern her now.

As the days turned to months, Diti carried Kashyapa's radiance within her, nurturing it in her womb. The power that grew inside her was vast, potent enough to outshine the very heavens. For a hundred years, she concealed that radiant energy, holding it within herself, until even the light of the Suns and stars dimmed before its brilliance.

The universe itself seemed to react to the force she carried. The sky darkened, the stars blinked less brightly, and even the *Lokapalas*—the guardians of the worlds—felt the shadow that now loomed over the cosmos. The disturbance was so great that it did not go unnoticed by the gods. The demigods, sages, and Maharishis, sensing the imbalance, gathered to discuss the strange darkness that had begun to veil the universe.

At last, their concerns led them to Brahma, the Creator. The gods approached him with their fears, their voices trembling with unease. 'Lord Brahma,' one of the sages said, 'there is a shadow over the cosmos. The light of the stars and Suns grows dim. What is the cause of this disturbance?'

Brahma, seated upon his lotus throne, listened patiently. His eyes, filled with the wisdom of countless aeons, held a knowing smile. 'Fear not,' he said, his voice steady and calm. 'This darkness you sense is not the end of all things, but the beginning of a great cycle. It is the unfolding of events set into motion long ago.'

The gods and sages watched him intently as he spoke, their fear mingling with curiosity.

'This shadow you feel,' Brahma continued, 'is the result of a curse. Long ago, the Sanat Kumaras—wise sages, sons of the divine—sought to enter the gates of Vaikuntha, the eternal abode of Vishnu. But as they approached, they were barred entry by the doorkeepers, Jaya and Vijaya, who, in their arrogance, failed to recognise the sanctity of the Kumaras. The sages, upset by this affront, cursed Jaya and Vijaya to be cast out of Vaikuntha and reborn into the mortal world as enemies of Vishnu.'

The gods listened with rapt attention as Brahma continued. 'The curse decreed that Jaya and Vijaya would be reborn three times, each time as demons of great power, destined to be slain by Vishnu himself. In each incarnation, they would rise to immense power, only to be destroyed by Vishnu, who would descend to restore balance to the world.'

The gods exchanged uneasy glances. The implications of Brahma's words were vast. The darkness that had begun to spread was the first sign of the curse's unfolding.

'Diti,' Brahma continued, 'bears the first incarnation of Jaya and Vijaya in her womb. Her sons, Hiranyaksha and Hiranyakashyapa, will be born as demons of terrible power. They will shake the very foundations of the earth and torment the innocent. But their reign will be short-lived, for Vishnu himself will descend to vanquish them.'

The gods nodded, understanding now the cosmic significance of the events that were about to unfold. Though the darkness loomed, it was not the end. It was merely part of the eternal cycle—destruction giving way to creation, death leading to rebirth.

As Diti carried her children within her, she remained proud of what she had conceived. She did not question the future that lay ahead, nor did she feel regret for the choices she had made. Her sons would be powerful, mighty beings who would command fear and respect. That was all that mattered.

The cosmic dance continued, and in its endless rhythm, the fate of gods, demons, and mortals was intertwined. Diti's sons grew within her as the universe darkened in anticipation of the storms they would bring. But through that darkness, the light of Vishnu waited, biding its time to descend once more and restore the balance of the world.

'In our first mortal lives, my brother Vijaya was born as Hiranyaksha. His strength and fury were unmatched; his ambition drove him to seek dominion over the earth and heavens. He challenged the very gods, driven by an insatiable thirst for power. But his hubris led him to confront Varaha, the boar incarnation of Vishnu. In his arrogance, he underestimated the divine, and Varaha vanquished him, restoring balance to the cosmos.

'Hiranyaksha's fall, like mine, was a testament to the folly of pride and the eternal truth that the cosmos has its order. Power without humility leads only to destruction. Let his end be a warning to all who seek to challenge the divine.'

– Ravana, Emperor of Lanka

FOUR

Hiranyaksha

Golden-eyed Terror

The cosmos trembled as Diti, after a hundred long years, finally gave birth to twin sons. From the moment the first cries of the newborns echoed across the realms, the universe itself seemed to recoil in terror. Earthquakes shattered the ground, fires sprang up spontaneously, and violent winds howled through the forests, uprooting trees and tossing them like toys. The skies, darkened by ominous clouds, were alive with flashes of lightning and the rumble of thunder, while the seas frothed and churned in uncontrollable fury. Nature itself rebelled against the existence of these creatures, signalling the magnitude of the evil they would soon unleash.

Sage Kashyapa, their father, stood solemnly before his newborn sons, his heart heavy with sadness. He looked upon the elder twin, whose eyes glistened with ambition and malevolence. 'You shall be called Hiranyakashyapa,' the sage declared, 'for you will hunger for gold, power, and dominion over the three worlds.'

Then, turning to the younger twin, Kashyapa's brow furrowed as he sensed an unbridled thirst for violence in the child. 'And you,' he continued, 'you shall be known as Hiranyaksha, the golden-eyed warrior, destined to revel in war and bloodshed.'

Hiranyaksha, from the moment he could walk, displayed an unparalleled love for cruelty. It was not enough for him to fight his enemies; he wanted to feel them break beneath his hands, to hear the snap of bones and the agonised screams of his victims. His favourite method of killing involved lifting his opponents by their throats, watching them struggle in his grasp, before crushing their windpipes with a casual squeeze. The thrill of their final, desperate gasps for air sent waves of ecstasy through the demon's twisted soul.

Even Hiranyakashyapa, ambitious and power-hungry as he was, found himself baulking at his brother's sheer delight in torment. Once, he watched Hiranyaksha dismember a foe piece by piece, drawing out the victim's suffering for hours, savouring every scream, every futile plea for mercy.

'Must you always play with your prey?' Shuddering, Hiranyakashyapa asked, a flicker of unease crossing his usually impassive face.

Hiranyaksha, grinning wildly, wiped the blood from his hands. 'What's the fun in a quick kill, brother? Where's the pleasure in that? Their suffering is a symphony, and I am its conductor.'

As the brothers grew, so did their thirst for domination. While Hiranyakashyapa sought to bring the three realms under his rule, Hiranyaksha was more interested in sowing chaos, destruction, and terror wherever he went. He roamed the heavens, the earth, and the netherworld, wielding his massive club and slaughtering any who dared to oppose him.

It wasn't long before even the gods began to fear the golden-eyed demon. Indra, the king of the heavens, grew so terrified of Hiranyaksha that he and the other gods went into hiding. Enraged by their cowardice, Hiranyaksha stormed through the heavens, dragging out lesser gods from their hiding places and smashing their bodies against the clouds. He revelled in their cries of agony, his laughter echoing through the skies like thunder.

Once, when Hiranyaksha found a group of demigods attempting to flee, he cornered them on the edge of a cliff. 'Run, little cowards,' he taunted, 'but know that death will find you all the same.' With a single swing of his club, he sent them plummeting into the abyss below, their shrieks of terror following them to their deaths.

Growing bored of hunting lesser gods, Hiranyaksha set his sights on a new target: Varuna, the Lord of the Waters. He plunged into the ocean's depths, seeking out Varuna's capital, Vibhavari, where he hoped to find a more satisfying challenge. As he approached the city, the aquatic creatures scattered in terror, aware of the dark presence that had entered their realm.

Bursting into Varuna's court, Hiranyaksha brandished his club and sneered at the god. 'I've heard tales of your power, Varuna,' he growled. 'Come, face me in battle if you dare!'

Varuna, a god of immense wisdom and calm, met Hiranyaksha's gaze without flinching. But instead of engaging in combat, Varuna gave a slow, thoughtful nod. 'I am too old for such sport, O son of Diti,' he said with a serene smile. 'But there is one who could give you the fight you seek—one whose strength even surpasses your own.'

Hiranyaksha's interest was piqued. 'And who might that be?'

'Lord Vishṇu,' Varuna replied. 'If it is a worthy adversary you seek, none is greater than he.'

Hiranyaksha's eyes gleamed at the mention of Vishnu. 'Very well,' he snarled. 'Vishnu will fall by my hand, and I shall claim dominion over the universe.'

Varuna watched the demon leave, a knowing glint in his eye. He had deflected Hiranyaksha's wrath towards a force far greater than the demon could comprehend. In Varuna's ancient wisdom, he knew that Vishnu, the Preserver of the Universe, would be the key to restoring balance.

However, even Hiranyaksha, drunk on his own power, knew that Vishnu was no ordinary foe. Seeking to ensure his victory, the demon embarked on a long and gruelling penance to gain the favour of Brahma, the Creator. His penance was so intense that the cosmos itself shook in response. Pleased with the demon's devotion, Brahma appeared before him. He said. 'Ask for a boon, and it shall be granted.'

Hiranyaksha, always strategic, made his demand. 'Grant me immortality, that I may never be defeated in battle.'

Brahma shook his head. 'Immortality is not mine to give, for even the greatest of beings must eventually fall.'

Undeterred, Hiranyaksha revised his request. 'Then grant that no god, man, or beast may ever defeat me.'

Brahma considered the request carefully, 'you must enumerate the beasts'. The demon was thorough, and began listing all manner of creatures in his demand. 'Very well,' Brahma said at last. 'You shall not be defeated by any god, man, or beast.'

In his arrogance, Hiranyaksha had forgotten one crucial detail. In his exhaustive list of creatures, he had overlooked the humble boar.

Brahma's boon granted, Hiranyaksha returned to the world with renewed confidence. Now believing himself to be invincible, his acts of cruelty became even more terrifying. No longer content to simply kill his enemies, he made a sport of their deaths. He would round up entire villages, forcing the people to watch as he slowly dismembered their loved ones. Their screams of horror filled the air, and Hiranyaksha would throw his head back in laughter, revelling in their suffering.

Even Hiranyakashyapa, who had grown accustomed to his brother's brutal ways, found himself disturbed by the sheer scale of Hiranyaksha's cruelty. 'Brother,' Hiranyakashyapa said one day, watching as Hiranyaksha toyed with a captured soldier, breaking his bones one by one, 'there is no need for such... excess.'

Hiranyaksha grinned, his golden eyes gleaming with malice. 'No need, perhaps,' he said, 'but where's the joy in restraint? Power is best savoured when it is feared.'

The fear Hiranyaksha cultivated soon spread across the three realms. Even the gods, who had once believed themselves untouchable, now cowered in the shadows, unwilling to face the golden-eyed terror.

But unknown to Hiranyaksha, his reign of destruction was soon to come to an end. For Vishnu, the Preserver, had been watching, and the time for his intervention was drawing near.

FIVE

The Wrath of Varaha

Theft of the Earth

As the tides of terror rose and engulfed the realms, Hiranyaksha's arrogance soared to unimaginable heights. He strode through the world with a sinister swagger, convinced of his invulnerability after receiving the boon from Brahma. No god, no man, no beast could bring him down—or so he believed. The very earth he walked on quivered beneath his feet, and the cosmos trembled in anticipation of the unspeakable horrors he left in his wake. Death followed wherever he went, but Hiranyaksha revelled in it. The cries of the suffering were his music, and the pain of others, his pleasure.

But the universe had other plans: for in the distant heavens, Vishnu stirred.

It was a day unlike any other when Hiranyaksha, bored of tormenting mere mortals, set his sights on an even grander scheme. Amidst the endless waters, he discovered Bhudevi, the Earth Goddess herself. The wicked grin that spread across his face in that moment sent chills through the realms.

'This will be my greatest prize,' Hiranyaksha mused

aloud as he lifted the Earth onto his shoulders, seeking to plunge her deep into the depths of *Rasatala*, the netherworld, drowning her in eternal darkness, knowing this would draw Vishnu out from his celestial abode. After all, Vishnu was the Preserver, sworn to protect the balance of the cosmos. Hiranyaksha believed that even the mighty Vishnu would be no match for the boon bestowed upon him by Brahma.

With unparalleled force, he plunged into the depths of the ocean, taking the Earth Goddess to the very bottom of the cosmic sea.

'I need not find Vishnu,' Hiranyaksha thought with a wicked grin, 'I will force him to come to me.'

The theft of the Earth from her rightful place caused the balance of the cosmos to shift violently. The skies darkened, the stars trembled, and the demigods, alarmed by these omens, realised something catastrophic was approaching. As they assembled, their voices filled the celestial hall with concern.

Varuna, the Lord of the Oceans, bowed his head gravely as he addressed the assembly. 'The Earth is lost, and the creature who holds it captive is the same one who defiled my domain,' Varuna said. 'Hiranyaksha will destroy everything if left unchecked'

Indra, king of the gods, stepped forward, his face ashen. 'Only one being can face Hiranyaksha in battle,' he declared. 'We must turn to Vishnu. Only he, in his infinite wisdom, can restore the balance.'

The gods gathered before Vishnu's abode, chanting

hymns of praise and pleading for his intervention. The Preserver, hearing their prayers, realised that the time had come to protect the world once again.

From the nostrils of Brahma, who sat in meditation on his lotus throne, emerged a tiny boar—no larger than a thumb. Yet within that minuscule form was contained the immeasurable power of Vishnu. The gods watched in awe as the little boar began to grow, his body swelling with divine might until he stood as tall as a mountain, towering above even the ocean waves.

Varaha, the boar incarnation of Vishnu, let out a thunderous roar that shook the heavens and the depths of the netherworld. His crimson eyes gleamed with fury, and his tusks, sharp and shining, glowed with the energy of the cosmos. His very presence radiated a force so immense that the oceans trembled before him.

Even mighty Varuna was moved by the sheer power of this form. 'O mighty Varaha,' Varuna called out, 'fold your mane, for its ferocity frightens the creatures of the deep!'

Varaha, hearing this, folded his fiery mane, his divine grace and power undiminished. From the heavens, Varaha plunged into the cosmic ocean, his immense body parting the waters as he dived deeper and deeper, searching for the lost Earth.

The oceans that had once trembled before Hiranyaksha now seemed to bow in reverence to the boar avatar of Vishnu, recognising the power of the divine within him. The sea creatures who had once fled from Hiranyaksha now swam in harmony, following Varaha as if understanding the cosmic significance of this moment.

At last, Varaha reached the dark, murky depths of *Rasatala*, where Hiranyaksha held the Earth captive. The demon had perched himself arrogantly, watching over his stolen prize, believing that no one could challenge him here in the depths of the netherworld.

But then, through the gloom, he saw it—two massive, glowing red eyes approaching him through the water. The darkness seemed to part as the hulking form of Varaha emerged, the water swirling violently in his wake.

Hiranyaksha had thought himself invincible, but even he felt a shiver of unease as he saw the dark shape of Varaha cutting through the waters. The boar's tusks gleamed as they glided through the depths, his form illuminated by the light of the universe itself.

'Who dares disturb my dominion?' Hiranyaksha bellowed, raising his club as he prepared for the fight. But even as he spoke, doubt crept into his voice. The force that approached was not like anything he had faced before.

The demon's confidence had once soared to unreachable heights. He had once torn apart his adversaries with his bare hands, laughing as they begged for mercy. His fingers had snapped bones like twigs, revelling in the shrill cries of the suffering. But now, as Hiranyaksha stood face to face with the astounding boar incarnation of Vishnu, terror surged through his veins.

Varaha roared—a sound so deafening, so full of divine

rage, that it tore through the waters like a thousand thunderclaps. The ocean itself seemed to recoil in fear. The very air around Hiranyaksha trembled, vibrating with the weight of Vishnu's fury. The demon, once eager for battle, now stood paralyzed, his limbs heavy as stone, his mind clouded with dread.

Varaha's massive form towered above him, the god's fiery mane crackling with an ethereal glow. His eyes were like molten coals, gleaming with a bloodlust that even the demon had never seen. His mammoth white tusks seemed to tear through the skies. For a moment, Hiranyaksha felt abject terror—a sensation that he had only seen fleetingly, in the eyes of his prey.

'You will die by my tusks, Hiranyaksha,' Varaha growled ominously, his voice low and menacing, echoing through the abyss. 'And the oceans will be stained with your blood.'

The battle raged for what seemed like an eternity, but with Varaha's ferocious assault, Hiranyaksha had been pushed to his limits. No longer was the demon the hunter, he was the prey: frantically swinging his great club in desperation hoping to stave off the inevitable. Every strike from the boar god's tusks sent waves of searing pain through his body. Every roar from Varaha shook the ocean, turning even the bravest creatures into quivering invertebrates.

Hiranyaksha's knees buckled as Varaha lunged at him, the tusks grazing his torso, carving deep gashes into his flesh. Blood poured from the demon's wounds, darkening the waters around him. His once-mighty arms, which had torn apart gods and men alike, now trembled with fear. He staggered backward, his golden eyes wide with terror.

Varaha's tusks plunged forward, impaling Hiranyaksha with a sickening crunch. The demon screamed—a high-pitched, agonised wail that echoed through the depths of the ocean. The pitiful wails of his torment were unlike any that had been heard before, for even the greatest of his own victims had not suffered so.

As Varaha twisted his tusks, driving them deeper into Hiranyaksha's chest, the demon's blood flowed in torrents. The once-blue waters of the cosmic ocean turned a ghastly crimson as his life force drained into the abyss. The sea creatures fled in terror from the red tide that consumed the depths.

The demon's body writhed on the tusks of Varaha, but the boar god showed no mercy. With a mighty heave, Varaha flung Hiranyaksha high into the air. The demon's body twisted grotesquely as he flew, his limbs contorted in unnatural angles, bones cracking under the force.

Hiranyaksha crashed into the ocean floor with a deafening impact, sinking deep into the mud and silt. His once-golden skin was now slick with blood, his eyes wide and glassy, as he struggled to draw breath. But Varaha was far from done.

In one final act of divine retribution, Varaha charged toward Hiranyaksha, who now lay gasping on the ocean floor. The demon raised a trembling hand, as if to beg for mercy, but his voice was hoarse, his words nothing more than a garbled plea.

'Mercy...' he croaked, barely audible.

But there was no mercy for the demon who had driven the Earth into chaos and terrorised the realms. With a final, thunderous roar, Varaha's tusks found their mark again, this time impaling Hiranyaksha through the throat. The demon gurgled, his body twitching in its death throes, before finally falling limp. His head lolled to the side, his once-fearsome eyes now glazed and lifeless.

The ocean trembled as Varaha roared and lifted the limp body of the demon with his tusks. Jerking his head slightly, the boar god hurled Hiranyaksha's crumpled form into the void. Hiranyaksha's blood, now mixed with the dark waters of the cosmic sea, was a horrifying, crimson vortex.

The mighty Varaha stood victorious, his breath heavy, his eyes still burning with divine wrath. The Earth was now his to save, but the oceans would forever be stained with the grim reminder of what happens to those who defy the will of the divine.

Varaha gently retrieved Bhudevi, the Earth Goddess. He rose to the surface with Bhudevi balanced upon his tusks. The once-clear waters now swirled in ghastly bloodied currents as the remnants of Hiranyaksha's body gradually disappeared into the depths. The gods watched in awe and horror, knowing that such fury had not been unleashed in ages. Vishnu, in his Varaha form, had not just defeated the demon—he had utterly annihilated him.

The roar of Varaha's final triumph echoed across the universe, a sound so fierce that the heavens themselves quivered. The Earth, nestled gently upon the tusks of the boar avatar, was lifted from the depths and restored to her rightful place.

But none, no gods, humans or beasts, would ever forget Hiranyaksha's gruesome end. His blood would remain, forever mingled with the waters, a warning to all who dare to challenge the might of the divine.

'In that first incarnation, I, Jaya, was Hiranyakashyapa, the asura king whose arrogance reached the heavens. I performed penances that shook the cosmos, earning boons that made me nearly invincible. I decreed that none could harm me—neither man nor beast, neither day nor night, neither inside nor outside. In my arrogance, I declared myself the ultimate power, demanding worship that rightfully belonged to Vishnu. My own son, Prahlada, remained devoted to the divine, despite my attempts to destroy his faith. In my defiance, I overlooked the omnipotence of the divine. Vishnu incarnated as Narasimha, a being neither man nor beast, and at twilight, in the threshold of my palace, he tore me asunder. My fall is a stark reminder that no boon can shield one from the consequences of hubris. The divine order is supreme, and even the greatest of powers must bow to it. Let my demise serve as a lesson: true power lies not in defiance but in understanding one's place within the cosmic order.'

—Ravana, Emperor of Lanka

SIX

The Rise of Hiranyakashyapa

The Impossible Boon

The death of Hiranyaksha reverberated through the very fabric of existence. The oceans still bore traces of his blood, and the skies remained clouded, reflecting the cosmic imbalance caused by the violent clash between the Daitya and Vishnu's Varaha form. But while the world moved on, the heart of Hiranyakashyapa, ruler of the Daityas, refused to heal. His beloved brother was gone, leaving behind a void no conquest or power could fill.

Seated upon his darkened throne in Trikuta, the vast Daitya capital, Hiranyakashyapa brooded. Trikuta was the jewel of his empire, nestled in the mountains, fortified and opulent, symbolising his absolute rule over his people. Yet, in this moment of loss, all its splendour seemed hollow. His mind churned with thoughts of vengeance and sorrow.

For days, he stared into the emptiness of the world without his brother, without Hiranyaksha, the one who had shared his ambitions, his dreams, and his battles. Hiranyaksha, the unstoppable warrior, the dauntless soul who had enjoyed battle as one would a feast, was now gone. Killed not by a fellow Daitya or even a god in a fair battle—but by a beast, by Vishnu himself in the form of a mere boar. The humiliation of it boiled within Hiranyakashyapa's heart.

His fists clenched as he muttered, 'You left me too soon, Hiranyaksha. Together, we would have ruled not just the earth, but all the worlds.' He reminisced bitterly over the days when his brother's strength had been his greatest asset, his sword arm, his unwavering protector.

Now, Vishnu stood triumphant. 'Vishnu...' he spat, the name searing his soul with loathing. The protector of the universe, the meddler, had dared to intervene in their affairs. But Hiranyakashyapa swore that Vishnu would not live to see his victory endure. This wasn't just about vengeance; it was about proving that the gods were not untouchable.

From a young age, Hiranyakashyapa had been driven by one singular ambition: domination. Raised in the lineage of Daityas, as the son of Diti and Kashyapa, his thirst for power was only rivalled by his intellect. While Hiranyaksha revelled in physical battles, Hiranyakashyapa sought a different kind of mastery—the mastery of the cosmos, to rule not only the physical realms but to subjugate even the gods to his will. His kingdom in Trikuta stood as a testament to his genius as a ruler and his might as a warrior.

As a youth, Hiranyakashyapa was a leader both feared and respected. Under his rule, Trikuta had grown from a stronghold of Daityas to a powerful capital that extended its influence over the earth and beyond. Yet, for all his conquests, he had always known that there was no ruler quite like Hiranyaksha. His brother's strength was not only physical but also emotional. In times of war, Hiranyaksha was the general who led his armies with unmatched fervour. In times of peace, he was the bulwark Hiranyakashyapa relied on, the one who would speak the truth when others dared not.

Hiranyakashyapa felt the loss like a phantom pain, a deep ache that gnawed at his soul. 'You were my sword, Hiranyaksha. Without you, my conquests would seem hollow.' He knew, however, that his path of dominion was not over. The grief he felt would fuel his next steps, and the memory of Hiranyaksha's death would give him the fire he needed to crush his enemies.

The skies outside his palace darkened, thunder rumbled, and lightning cracked as Hiranyakashyapa stood atop the palace walls, looking out over his kingdom. His eyes were wild with fury, his chest heaving with the weight of his anger. The Daityas, his people, watched in silence, afraid to approach their king in his time of mourning. Even his queen, Kayadhu, stayed away.

Consumed by thoughts of revenge, Hiranyakashyapa summoned his advisors. They gathered in his throne room, a dark chamber adorned with Daitya banners and war trophies from conquests of the past. Flames flickered in the sconces, casting deep shadows across the faces of the Daitya chieftains.

'We are now leaderless, my lord,' one of his ministers

dared to speak. 'Hiranyaksha was our greatest warrior. The gods rejoice at his death.'

Hiranyakashyapa's eyes, now blazing with fury, silenced the room. 'The gods celebrate too early.' His voice was cold and venomous. 'They think this is their victory, but they have only ignited a fire they will soon regret. They may have killed my brother, but I will kill their very protector—Vishnu. I will tear the heavens apart to find him. Vishnu will pay for this. I will not rest until the three worlds tremble beneath my feet, and Vishnu himself begs for mercy,' he vowed.

The gathered Daityas murmured, their apprehension growing in the face of their lord's wrath. 'We will build an empire that stretches beyond the heavens,' Hiranyakashyapa continued. 'No god, no mortal, no demon will stand against me. But to do this, I need power greater than even the gods.' He knew that to challenge Vishnu, to face the gods and win, he would need immense resolve. The creator had bestowed boons upon him and his brother before; he would now seek the greatest boon of all—immortality.

Determined to claim dominion over the cosmos and avenge his brother, Hiranyakashyapa embarked on a perilous journey to perform penance, seeking the favour of Brahma, his own great-grandfather, creator of the universe. The Mandara Mountains, towering and remote, would be the altar for his immense sacrifice.

He began his austerities, standing on one foot, his arms outstretched towards the heavens, chanting the sacred mantras with a single focus: to summon Brahma and demand a boon. His penance was no ordinary prayer; it was a full embodiment of the Daitya's will. His very presence caused the mountains to tremble, the skies to darken, and the winds to howl in anguish. Years passed, and his power grew, his body weakening as his spirit strengthened.

The gods, sensing the growing threat, became deeply disturbed. They had seen such penance before. But, with the unfolding events came an opportunity.

In the heavenly realm, Indra, king of the gods, watched Hiranyakashyapa's asceticism with growing concern. The balance of power was shifting, and he knew that something had to be done to stop the Daitya. 'We must strike now,' he declared to the Devas. 'While he is consumed in his meditation, we will attack his kingdom and cripple him before he can gain strength.'

With swift precision, Indra led his forces in an assault on Hiranyakashyapa's kingdom—Trikuta. The Daityas, without their king and leader, were no match for Indra's armies. Kayadhu, Hiranyakashyapa's queen, was taken captive by Indra, who sought to use her as leverage to keep the Daitya king in check.

As Kayadhu was dragged from her home in chains, she clutched her stomach protectively. Unknown to her captors, she was carrying the child of Hiranyakashyapa—a child who would one day shape the destiny of the universe.

As Indra's army made their way to the heavens with

their captive, they were met by Narada, the wandering sage. Narada, known for his wisdom and foresight, intervened upon seeing the pregnant Kayadhu in chains.

'Indra,' Narada said, raising his hand to stop the divine procession, 'Release this woman. She has done no wrong.'

Indra, though suspicious of Narada's motives, respected the sage's wisdom. 'She is the wife of Hiranyakashyapa,' he argued. 'Her very presence is a threat to us all.'

Narada confronted Indra. 'She is with child. Release her.'

Reluctantly, Indra released Kayadhu into Narada's care. 'I will hold you accountable for this, Narada,' he warned. 'If Hiranyakashyapa's fury returns to haunt us, the blame will be yours.'

Narada smiled, his serene demeanour unshaken. 'The child within her will change the course of history. Have faith in the ways of the universe, Indra.'

Narada took Kayadhu to his ashram, where she was treated with kindness and dignity. As the days passed, Narada spoke to her of Vishnu, the protector of the universe, and told her tales of his glory. Though she carried the seed of a tyrant within her, her mind was filled with thoughts of righteousness and virtue.

Brahma, moved by Hiranyakashyapa's sheer dedication, appeared before him, radiant with divine light.

'Hiranyakashyapa,' Brahma spoke, his voice echoing like thunder, 'What do you desire? You have performed great penance, and I am pleased. Name your wish, and

I shall grant it, as far as the universe permits.'

With his mind clouded by grief and rage, Hiranyakashyapa stood before the radiant form of Brahma, ready to demand his place above the gods themselves. His meditation had paid off, and now, Brahma, the creator, stood ready to grant him his desires. But Hiranyakashyapa knew better than to ask outright for immortality, a boon denied even to the greatest beings. His intellect, sharpened by years of ambition, searched for a way to defy death without breaking the cosmic laws.

Hiranyakashyapa's lips curled into a faint smile, his eyes gleaming with wicked purpose. He folded his hands in mock reverence and bowed his head. 'O Lord Brahma, I have no wish for immortality, as I know even you cannot grant that.'

Brahma nodded. 'Indeed, none in creation are beyond death.'

Hiranyakashyapa continued, his voice steady. 'Then grant me this instead: I wish that no being you have created—neither gods, men, nor animals—shall have the power to slay me.'

Brahma hesitated, sensing the cunning behind the request, but his vow to reward the Daitya's devotion bound him. '*Tathastu.* Let it be so,' Brahma decreed.

Hiranyakashyapa, feeling the weight of the universe tilting in his favour, pressed on. 'Further, I ask that I may not meet my end during the hours of daylight nor in the dead of night.'

Again, Brahma assented. '*Tathastu.*'

'And make it so that I cannot die on earth nor in the heavens, nor in any realm between them.'

Brahma's face remained impassive as he granted the boon. *'Tathastu.'*

Hiranyakashyapa's eyes gleamed with malicious glee. His next words came swiftly, calculated. 'O Lord, ensure that no weapon of man, god, or demon—not anything living or non-living—can be used to kill me.'

Brahma, sensing the danger in granting such unchecked power, hesitated but could not retract his promise. *'Tathasthu,'* he repeated once more.

The final request came with a cruel smile. 'Finally, I ask that I may not be killed inside any dwelling nor outside. Let there be no place where I can be touched by death.'

For the last time, Brahma's voice echoed with his decree. *'Tathastu.'*

A deep, sinister satisfaction filled Hiranyakashyapa's heart. His requests, each carefully crafted to exploit the loopholes of fate, were granted. Brahma's light began to fade, his form withdrawing from the physical world.

As he disappeared, he spoke one last time, his voice tinged with an enigmatic warning. 'The boons you have asked for are given, but remember, Hiranyakashyapa, no power is beyond the balance of the universe.'

Hiranyakashyapa bowed low, masking his contempt. 'I thank you, great Brahma, for the boon you have bestowed upon me. With it, the universe itself shall bow before me.'

As Hiranyakashyapa descended the Mandara Mountains, his mind was already racing with thoughts of revenge. He was no longer the grieving brother but a being of pure wrath imbued with near-immortality, untouchable by gods, men, or beasts. Vishnu, who had slain Hiranyaksha in his boar avatar, would soon taste defeat at his hands.

But first, there was the matter of his city—Trikuta. As he neared the foothills, word reached him that Indra, the King of the Devas, had launched a cowardly assault on his capital while he was deep in meditation. The city had been razed, its towering structures brought to dust, and his beloved queen, Kayadhu, had been taken captive.

Hiranyakashyapa's eyes burned with fury. 'Indra,' he snarled, his voice trembling with rage, 'you dare to strike at me in my moment of grief? You think you can hold my wife to ransom? I shall burn your heavens to the ground and string your entrails from the stars!'

His chieftains, who had come to greet him at the base of the mountain, trembled before their king's wrath. But Hiranyakashyapa was not done. 'Prepare for war,' he commanded. 'We march on Indra's realm, and not one of them shall live to tell the tale.'

As the Daitya armies mobilised, Hiranyakashyapa's mind seethed with plans of vengeance. But unknown to him, a greater plan was already in motion. His wife, Kayadhu carried within her a child whose destiny would one day shake the very foundations of Hiranyakashyapa's empire. Yet for now, the child remained unknown, even to the father.

In the celestial realm, the Devas watched in apprehension as Hiranyakashyapa, fuelled by grief and the power of Brahma's boons, marshalled his forces for a war that would shake the heavens. Sitting upon his throne in Amaravati, Indra's confidence began to waver as he realised the storm he had provoked. Even his advisors were not immune to the creeping dread that now filled their halls.

'He will come for us,' Indra admitted quietly to his inner council. 'I thought taking his city would weaken him, but I fear I've only stoked his anger.'

The Devas, who had watched with satisfaction as Vishnu defeated Hiranyaksha, now realised they had made a dangerous enemy of his brother. None could match the boons Hiranyakashyapa had received, and none among them had the strength to challenge him.

Unbeknownst to Hiranyakashyapa, the wheels of fate were turning elsewhere. In the heavens, Vishnu watched from his cosmic abode, knowing full well that the time for another confrontation was approaching. After the Varaha avatar, he had withdrawn into deep contemplation, aware that the Daityas would not rest after Hiranyaksha's fall.

But Vishnu, ever the preserver, remained patient. While Hiranyakashyapa's power grew, so too did the forces of balance. The cosmos, though swayed by Hiranyakashyapa's ambition, would not allow chaos to reign for long.

SEVEN

The Tyranny of the Daitya King

The Rebel Son

Time had passed since Hiranyakashyapa had returned to his kingdom, strengthened by the boons granted by Brahma and driven by an insatiable thirst for vengeance. As his empire grew, so did his lust for power, and soon the Daitya king's ambitions had no limits. Hiranyakashyapa, once the bereaved brother mourning Hiranyaksha, was now consumed by darkness, anger, and pride. His kingdom of Trikuta, rebuilt from the ashes of Indra's attack, now stood as the epicentre of his tyranny, radiating fear across all three worlds.

Unknown to Hiranyakashyapa, during his time of austerity in the mountains, after Indra had captured his wife Kayadhu and Narada offered her refuge in his ashram, his son Prahlada, while in Kayadhu's womb, was in the constant presence of Narada's teachings. Day and night, the sage extolled the virtues of Vishnu, his stories of divine compassion, and his protection of the universe.

Kayadhu, worried about her husband's wrath, sat impassively. And yet, she unconsciously absorbed these divine teachings. However, it was the unborn child who truly imbibed them. The vibrations of devotion reached the child's consciousness, shaping Prahlada into a future devotee of Vishnu. Even before he saw the world, Prahlada was bound to Vishnu, his mind purified by Narada's discourses on dharma, compassion, and the cosmic order.

This early immersion into divine wisdom would lay the foundation for Prahlada's unshakable faith, a faith that would stand against the terrifying wrath of his father. While Hiranyakashyapa sought to impose his will as supreme, growing within his own bloodline was the seed of rebellion—one rooted in devotion to the very god he sought to destroy.

With his newfound invincibility, Hiranyakashyapa declared himself lord of the universe. No longer would the Devas rule the heavens, no longer would men or gods bow to Vishnu. The Daitya king's will was now the supreme law, and any deviation from his commands was met with cruelty and swift punishment.

Hiranyakashyapa was no longer merely a king or a conqueror; he was a tyrant. And like all tyrants, he demanded absolute loyalty. His fury was matched only by his cruelty, and it soon became clear that there were no lengths to which he would not go to maintain his rule. His orders were unquestionable, and those who dared to defy him were met with horrific ends.

One of Hiranyakashyapa's earliest decrees after his rise to power was the total ban on the worship of any deity other than himself. The edict spread like wildfire, carried by his soldiers and enforced with unrelenting cruelty.

The priests who once served the temples of Vishnu were forced to pledge their allegiance to the Daitya king and dragged from their sanctuaries and publicly humiliated upon resistance. Those who refused to comply were tortured and executed in front of their congregations as a warning to others. Entire villages were massacred if even a single inhabitant dared to take Vishnu's name and temples were razed to the ground. In the capital, massive pyres of sacred texts were burned, the smoke choking the air with the smell of desecration.

'Vishnu!' he bellowed from his throne, his voice echoing throughout his court. 'He who slayed my brother with deceit and cowardice! He who hides in the shadows, pretending to be the protector of the universe! Let it be known: from this day forth, Vishnu is an enemy to all creation. No prayers shall reach him; no temple shall bear his image. I alone am to be worshipped as the ruler of all worlds!'

From the heavenly realms to the lowliest village on earth, statues and images of Hiranyakashyapa were erected. All were commanded to worship him as the supreme being, and a decree was passed that anyone caught praying to any other deity, especially Vishnu, would be subject to unimaginable punishment.

Yet, despite the violence, some still clung to their faith in the preserver god. They prayed in secret, lighting oil lamps in the dead of night, hiding their devotion behind locked doors. But Hiranyakashyapa's spies were ever-watchful, and those who defied him were soon discovered and brought to their knees. The Asura soldiers roamed the lands, dragging dissenters to their doom. Entire families were executed for the crime of secretly praying to Vishnu. Children were torn from their mothers' arms, men were killed in front of their families, and even the gods trembled, knowing they could not intervene under Hiranyakashyapa's reign. The rivers ran red with blood, and the once-vibrant earth turned into a desolate landscape of corpses and ash.

Hiranyakashyapa's creative cruelty knew no bounds. He began to mirror all that Hiranyaksha used to take pleasure in. The torture chambers beneath his palace reverberated with the screams of the defiant. Dissidents who failed to obey his edicts were brought to his court and executed in gruesome ways. He delighted in hearing the agonising screams of his enemies, often devising elaborate methods of torture himself. Whether it was crushing bones beneath massive iron hammers or slow dismemberment, being thrown into pits of fire, bones shattered one by one, or being skinned alive, each punishment was a spectacle for the court to witness, a reminder of the absolute power of the Daitya king.

In the throne room of his palace, Hiranyakashyapa sat atop a mountain of skulls, his gaze cold and cruel. Every whisper of defiance only fuelled his wrath further, as he ruthlessly maintained his stranglehold over the universe. His kingdom had transformed into a nightmarish domain of fear and bloodshed, where no one could escape the anger of the self-proclaimed god-king.

Despite this realm of fear, an unexpected defiance began to brew—a defiance from within his own bloodline. Prahlada, Hiranyakashyapa's beloved son, was raised in the asura court with every advantage of wealth and power, taught to follow in the tyrant's footsteps. Hiranyakashyapa, proud of his lineage, saw his son as the future of his reign, and hoped to mould him into the perfect ruler, a mirror of his own ambition.

As a child, Prahlada was sent to the asura sage Shukracharya, along with other young students, to be educated in the ways of ruling, warfare, and devotion to Hiranyakashyapa. But something curious began to happen. As the other students learned to praise their king, Prahlada's heart wandered elsewhere. Instead of venerating his father as the supreme lord, he would whisper the name Vishnu—the very god his father so detested.

One day, during a grand assembly, Hiranyakashyapa asked his son with fatherly pride, 'Prahlada, my son, what have you learned from your studies?' He expected his son to shower him with praises, as all others did. But instead, Prahlada's innocent voice rang out with words that sent a chill through the hall.

'I have learned that the greatest one is Vishnu, the Lord who preserves all creation.'

Hiranyakashyapa froze, his face darkening. He could not believe what he was hearing. 'What did you say?' he growled, leaning forward on his throne, his eyes wide with fury.

But Prahlada, unaware of the storm he had just unleashed, repeated himself, this time with even more conviction. 'Vishnu is the true lord, father. It is to him that we all must offer our prayers, not to any king or mortal being.'

A hush fell over the assembly. The Daitya lords stared in shock at the young boy, while Hiranyakashyapa's face turned crimson with rage. 'Vishnu!' he spat, standing from his throne. 'How dare you utter the name of that vile god in my presence!' His voice thundered through the hall.

'Take the boy away!' he ordered, his hands trembling with anger. 'Send him back to his teachers. This insolence must be corrected. Let Shukracharya straighten him out!'

Prahlada was returned to the care of Shukracharya's assistants, who took their role seriously, teaching him with renewed vigour the ways of the asuras and the importance of reverence for his father. But despite their best efforts, Prahlada remained steadfast in his devotion to Vishnu. Every lesson, every mantra taught to him, was drowned out by his unshakable faith in the Lord of Preservation.

What was even more infuriating for the teachers was the influence Prahlada began to exert on his fellow students. In secret, Prahlada would gather the other asura children and teach them about the greatness of Vishnu, urging them to abandon the path of darkness and embrace the light. One by one, the children, captivated by Prahlada's sincerity, began to question the ways of their fathers and the cruel reign of Hiranyakashyapa.

It wasn't long before word of this silent rebellion reached the Daitya king's ears. At first, Hiranyakashyapa dismissed the rumours. 'He is just a child,' he scoffed. 'This will pass.' But as more reports came in of students openly refusing to bow to him and instead singing hymns to Vishnu, Hiranyakashyapa's anger grew.

He summoned Prahlada again. 'Have you learned nothing, boy?' he demanded, his voice shaking with fury. 'You defy me, even after I have given you every comfort and privilege?'

Prahlada stood before his father, his expression calm but resolute. 'Father, I do not defy you. I love you. But Vishnu is the lord of all creation. It is he who rules the universe, not any man or demon.'

Hiranyakashyapa's patience snapped. 'This is not love!' he roared. 'This is betrayal! I will not have my own son worshipping my enemy!'

In a fit of rage, Hiranyakashyapa ordered his guards to take the boy to the darkest dungeons, where he would be left to reconsider his loyalties.

Kayadhu stood alone in the palace chamber, her heart heavy with worry. Hiranyakashyapa stormed in, his face dark with anger.

'I have had enough of that boy's rebellion,' Hiranyakashyapa thundered. 'His defiance is a poison spreading among our people. If he does not understand who his true god and master is, then the dungeons will teach him respect.'

Kayadhu's face grew pale. She clasped her hands together, stepping closer to him, her voice barely above a whisper. 'My lord, he is but a child—our youngest son. He doesn't understand the forces and feuds that rule the world. His praise of Vishnu, misguided as it is, comes from innocence. Please, I beg you… spare him the terrible darkness of the dungeons.'

Hiranyakashyapa's eyes blazed with contempt. 'Innocence? Is it innocence to sing praises of the one who killed one's own kin? This is not a child's folly, Kayadhu. This is open betrayal!' He clenched his fists. 'To speak the name of Vishnu in my kingdom, let alone among the children of the asura race, is a disgrace.'

Kayadhu's voice shook as she pleaded, 'He is still our son, my lord. Can we not guide him with patience? Can we not show him the strength of the Daitya way without such cruelty?'

'Son?' Hiranyakashyapa spat. 'No son of mine would betray his father's honour and sing paeans to our greatest enemy. To defile his own bloodline with the name of that cowardly god? Such a child is no son of mine! I disown him.' His words cut through Kayadhu like a knife, and she took a step back, stifling a sob. She could feel his fury radiating, an unforgiving force.

Seeing her struggle, Hiranyakashyapa's expression softened momentarily, but only with disgust. 'And you, Kayadhu—why do you speak for that treacherous boy? Have you, too, been seduced by the enemy's name?'

Kayadhu shook her head, tears welling in her eyes. 'No, my lord. I would never betray you. But is it wrong to love our son? To fear for his safety?' Her mind drifted to memories she kept buried: her father Jambha, the great Naga, humiliated and defeated by Hiranyakashyapa when he had seized her from her home. From that day, she had lived only to serve her husband, enduring his temper and his wars. But must she now bear the horror of watching him destroy their own child?

Hiranyakashyapa's eyes narrowed as he took in her trembling form. 'Weakness! If your heart bleeds for him, steel it. We are Daityas, Diti's offspring. We harden our sons through rigorous training. If they cannot handle the regimen, they are better off dead! The dungeons will teach him submission to my way. He will come to his senses—or fall by his own folly. I will not have this disgrace spread through my kingdom.'

Kayadhu knew better than to contradict him when his rage was so fierce. She lowered her gaze, though her voice was a quiet plea. 'Then… then please let me go to him, my lord. Let me speak to him in the dungeons. He is young. Surely he must be afraid.'

Hiranyakashyapa paused, an unreadable look in his eyes, and finally gave a dismissive wave. 'Do as you wish. Go to him, but understand this: if he speaks of Vishnu again, I will make him suffer worse.'

Kayadhu bowed, her heart heavy with despair. 'Thank you, my lord,' she whispered. And as Hiranyakashyapa strode out, leaving her alone in the vast chamber, she whispered softly to herself, 'I only pray that the darkness does not consume him… or you.'

Days turned into weeks, and yet Prahlada remained unbroken. Word spread throughout Trikuta that even in the depths of the dungeons, the boy continued to chant Vishnu's name, his faith unshaken. Hiranyakashyapa, once hopeful that his son would return to his senses, now found himself the subject of ridicule among the Daitya lords.

The murmurs of discontent grew louder. 'The mighty Hiranyakashyapa made a fool of by his own son!' they would whisper behind his back.

Hiranyakashyapa's patience finally snapped. In a burst of rage, he called his court together and declared that Prahlada must die. No longer was the boy merely a rebellious child; in Hiranyakashyapa's eyes, he had become a threat to the very stability of his rule.

'How dare my own son speak the name of my greatest enemy?' Hiranyakashyapa roared to his advisors. 'How dare he defy me, the ruler of the universe? He has chosen Vishnu over his own father, and for that, he must be destroyed.'

The court fell into uneasy silence. To kill one's own child was a terrible act, but none dared to oppose the Daitya king. They knew that Hiranyakashyapa's wrath would be far worse than any moral hesitation. And so, the order was given—Prahlada would face execution.

EIGHT

The Rage of Narasimha

Trials of Prahlada

The great city of Trikuta had seen many horrors under the rule of Hiranyakashyapa, but none would compare to the punishment he devised for his son, Prahlada. The Daitya king, having issued the decree of death for the boy, sought to make an example of him that would haunt the hearts of those who dared to utter the name of Vishnu. The torments Prahlada was about to endure would be unmatched in their cruelty.

Hiranyakashyapa ordered his soldiers to throw Prahlada into a pit filled with venomous snakes, and the serpents struck again and again, sinking their fangs deep into the boy's flesh. Yet, in a stunning display of what could only be described as divine intervention, the poison did not harm him. The snakes recoiled, as if repelled by an unseen force, and Prahlada stood amidst them, unharmed.

The boy closed his eyes and whispered, 'Vishnu is with me.'

Hiranyakashyapa watched from afar, his fists clenched. He had expected to see his son writhe in pain, to hear his cries for mercy, but there was nothing.

'How?' Hiranyakashyapa growled. 'How does he survive?'

Infuriated by this failure, Hiranyakashyapa then commanded that his son be trampled under the feet of wild elephants. The great beasts, their tusks gleaming like spears, were driven into a maddened frenzy by their keepers. They charged at Prahlada, their massive feet set to crush him into the dust. But as they approached, the ground beneath the boy seemed to harden, as though Vishnu himself had intervened. The elephants stopped just short of the child, their rage inexplicably subdued.

Frustrated and enraged, Hiranyakashyapa's ordered that Prahlada be thrown from the highest cliffs of Mount Trikuta, the jagged rocks below hungry for blood. Yet even as the boy fell, a gust of wind, unnatural in its timing and force, seemed to cradle him, lowering him gently to the ground.

Next, Prahlada was bound in iron chains and submerged in a cauldron of boiling oil, its heat intense enough to melt steel. The court waited for the boy to scream in agony, but once again, the impossible happened. The oil bubbled and hissed, but Prahlada remained untouched, standing calmly amidst the deadly heat.

Over and over again, Hiranyakashyapa's most gruesome punishments failed. Whether by fire, sword, or poison, nothing could harm Prahlada.

The Daitya king's frustration mounted, his fury now almost animalistic. 'I will not be mocked by a child! I will not be mocked by this... Vishnu! I shall end this myself.'

The king, determined to break his son's spirit, ordered a massive pyre to be built. Holika, Hiranyakashyapa's sister, had been granted a boon that no fire could harm her and thus, was summoned.

'Holika, take the boy in your lap and sit in the centre of the pyre. Your boon will ensure that he is reduced to ash while you remain unharmed.'

'Set the pyre ablaze,' roared Hiranyakashyapa, 'and let us see if his Vishnu will save him from the flames!' Holika walked up to the boy, picked him up and began to move towards the hot flames. Prahlada showed no resistance.

As the fire roared and crackled, Holika took Prahlada in her lap and sat upon the pyre. The flames rose high into the sky, their heat scorching the air around them. However, as the fire engulfed them, it was Holika who began to scream piteously. The flames did not touch Prahlada, but they consumed her entirely, as if her boon had been revoked by the very universe. Her screams echoed across the palace grounds, and soon, ashes were all that was left of her.

Hours later, as the fires died out, the boy was found sitting still, his eyes closed in prayer, unscathed. Hiranyakashyapa's face twisted in disbelief. 'This is impossible!' he snarled. 'How can he survive?'

As the court watched these repeated miracles, whispers began to spread among Hiranyakashyapa's own people. Some murmured that perhaps Vishnu was protecting the boy after all. But the Daitya king would not entertain such thoughts. His fury was now beyond control, his mind clouded by rage. It was clear that no earthly force could kill Prahlada, but Hiranyakashyapa was determined. He would take matters into his own hands.

Hiranyakashyapa stormed through his palace, his eyes burning with the fires of vengeance. His once-glorious empire now felt like a prison, his authority mocked by the gods and by his own flesh and blood. It was time to end this rebellion once and for all, by his own hands if necessary.

He dragged Prahlada to the throne room, the place where his rule over the universe had once seemed absolute. Throwing the boy to the ground, he drew closer, his voice shaking with fury. 'Where is your Vishnu now, Prahlada?' he bellowed, his eyes gleaming with hatred. 'You speak of him constantly, but where is he? Is he here? Does he hide in the walls? In the heavens? Tell me, where does he dwell!'

Calm and resolute, Prahlada looked up at his father and spoke softly, 'He is everywhere, Father. He is within me. He is within you. He is in this very room.'

Hiranyakashyapa's rage boiled over. Grabbing his mace, he stormed toward a massive stone pillar in the throne room, his voice thunderous, echoing across the chamber. 'If your Vishnu is everywhere, let him appear now, from this pillar!'

With a roar of fury, Hiranyakashyapa lifted his mace high above his head and struck the pillar with all his strength.

The blow echoed like thunder through the palace,

and the pillar cracked. For a moment, there was only silence. Then, with a sound like the tearing of the earth itself, the pillar shattered. From within its depths came a deafening roar, a roar so terrible that it shook the very foundations of the universe.

Emerging from the broken stone was a figure unlike anything the world had ever seen—a being that defied all logic, all reason. It was neither man nor beast, but a monstrous half-man, half-lion form: Narasimha, the terrible avatar of Vishnu. His face was a terrifying leonine visage, with eyes that burned with the intensity of a thousand suns, and a mane that seemed to flicker as flames of the apocalypse. His massive claws, sharp as the finest blades, gleamed in the dim light.

Hiranyakashyapa, for the first time in his life, felt fear. Real, gut-wrenching fear.

'Who—what—are you?' he stammered.

The tyrant who had never known defeat, who had believed himself invincible, stood paralyzed before this terrible being. Narasimha's towering form seemed to blot out the heavens, his presence radiating a fierce, otherworldly power.

Narasimha was no god of mercy. He was rage incarnate, the embodiment of divine wrath, and as he stepped toward Hiranyakashyapa, his steps seemed to echo across eternity. The Daitya king tried to lift his mace, but his arms shook with terror. Before he could react, Narasimha seized him by the throat with one of his mighty, clawed hands.

The king, once proud ruler of the three worlds, dangled helplessly in the beast's grip. Narasimha's face was a mask of unholy wrath, his fangs bared in bloodlust. And with a snarl that could split the sky, Narasimha roared.

The Daitya king struggled, but it was as if the strength of the universe was against him. Narasimha dragged him to the threshold of the palace, where the setting sun cast a strange twilight over the scene—neither day nor night, neither inside nor outside.

'You asked for a boon, Hiranyakashyapa,' the god growled, his voice a powerful, thundering rumble. 'No man, no beast, no weapon could harm you. But I am neither. And now, you shall meet your end.'

Hiranyakashyapa's last breath rattled in his throat as Narasimha raised him high into the air and then slammed him down onto his knees. With a ferocious snarl, Narasimha drove his claws into Hiranyakashyapa's chest, ripping through flesh and bone as though they were nothing. The king screamed in agony, but there was no escape. Narasimha tore him apart, piece by piece, his bloodied claws gleaming in the dying light. The Daitya king's entrails spilled onto the floor, and Narasimha, with savage glee, fashioned a garland from them, draping it around his neck in a grotesque mockery of Hiranyakashyapa's once-great power.

Hiranyakashyapa's screams echoed through the palace, but no one dared intervene. The mighty king, now reduced to a quivering, bloodied husk, was no match for the primal force that had been unleashed upon him. Narasimha's claws raked through his chest, his ribs snapping like dry twigs. The beast-god roared once more, as though the act of consuming Hiranyakashyapa's flesh brought him some cosmic satisfaction.

With a final, brutal motion, Narasimha tore open the Daitya king's chest, his claws sinking into the still-beating heart. He lifted the bloodied organ to his lips, the dark blood running down his chin as he feasted on the very essence of the tyrant who had defied the gods. The air was thick with the scent of blood and death, the earth beneath Narasimha soaked in red.

In the final moments of his life, Hiranyakashyapa's eyes, wide with terror, met those of the monstrous god. There was no mercy, no reprieve. In that terrible gaze, Hiranyakashyapa saw the full power of the universe—the fury of creation and destruction made manifest.

Hiranyakashyapa's life ebbed away as Narasimha dismembered him, savouring each drop of his blood. And then, in a single, violent motion, Narasimha ended the Daitya king's life, rending his body and casting the remains into the void.

Hiranyakashyapa's body was ravaged beyond recognition, his remains torn and devoured by the feral might of Narasimha. Blood ran like rivers, staining the palace grounds a deep crimson, pooling beneath the shattered pillar from which the avatar had emerged. It was a horrific spectacle—Narasimha, a vision of primal ferocity, stood triumphantly over the remains of the once-mighty Daitya king, his terrible roar echoing through the heavens.

In that moment, the reign of Hiranyakashyapa ended, not with a whimper, but with a roar that would be remembered for all eternity. The lord of terror had met his match, and the balance of the cosmos was restored, through the blood-soaked hands of Narasimha, the terrible god who had walked the earth, if only for a moment, to exact vengeance.

The asuras and demigods, who had gathered to witness the scene, stood frozen in terror and awe. Even the most hardened warriors of the Daitya army could not bear the sight; some fell to their knees, while others fled the palace, their minds shattered by the sheer terror of the spectacle.

As Narasimha sat atop Hiranyakashyapa's lifeless body, the terms of Brahma's boon to the Daitya king were fulfilled to the letter. *Neither man nor beast*—Narasimha was a creature beyond either. *Neither day nor night*—the twilight sky framed the moment perfectly. *Neither inside nor outside*—the threshold of the palace was neither one nor the other. *And, by no weapon forged by man or god*—Narasimha had ripped him apart with his claws.

The earth seemed to tremble in the presence of Narasimha's fury. His blazing eyes, still hungry for destruction, scanned the room. His wrath had not yet been satiated. His divine power was too great for mortal minds to comprehend, and for a moment, it seemed as if Narasimha would not stop with Hiranyakashyapa. His ferocity might consume the entire universe.

But then, from the shadows, emerged a small, unassuming figure—Prahlada, the boy who had defied his father's tyranny with unwavering devotion to Vishnu.

As he approached Narasimha, there was no fear in his eyes, no hesitation in his steps. The monstrous god, still covered in Hiranyakashyapa's blood, turned his terrible gaze upon the child.

'My lord, please calm your fury. The tyrant is gone, and justice is served. Spare the world from your anger, as you have spared me from harm.'

Narasimha, breathing heavily, slowly lowered his gaze, the fire in his eyes dimming. He saw not a mere boy before him but the embodiment of devotion, a soul untouched by the corruption of the world. In the presence of such purity, Narasimha's anger melted away. He reached out one great clawed hand and gently touched the top of Prahlada's head, a gesture of blessing from the same claws that had torn his father apart.

The atmosphere shifted. The terror of the moment passed, and the universe let out a sigh of relief. The demigods who had watched the scene in awe came forward now, bowing low to Narasimha, but it was clear the true reverence was for Prahlada, the boy whose faith had triumphed over the greatest evil.

As brutal and terrifying as Narasimha's justice was, it was not without purpose. Hiranyakashyapa's reign of terror had been brought to an end, and the world had been saved from further torment. The natural order, once disrupted by the Daitya king's unholy ambitions, had been restored, and the universe could once again breathe freely.

For though the world may fall into darkness, though

tyranny may rise and the innocent may suffer, the universe has a way of righting itself. And in the end, the forces of justice, however terrifying they may be, will always prevail.

'Ah, mortals and gods who stand witness to my fall, heed my words once more, for the journey of my soul is not yet over. As I, Ravana, breathe my final breaths on this battlefield, a vision stirs within me, one that stretches beyond the bounds of this life, beyond Lanka, beyond even the present. I am blessed to see through time itself, and what I see ahead is a fate yet to unfold, a destiny that binds me and my brother Vijaya to a new cycle of birth and death.

'In a future age, when the yugas have turned and the Dwapara Yuga has dawned, I will be born once again. This time, as Shishupal, a Vrishni prince, and my brother Vijaya, reborn as Dantavakra, will walk the earth with me. We will be cousins to Lord Vishnu, who shall incarnate as Krishna, yet we will not recognise him as the divine. Our hearts, consumed by envy and rage, will see him only as a rival, a mere mortal to be outdone.

'How strange and bitter is the irony—once his loyal servant, now blinded by jealousy, I shall defy him again, failing to see the very god I once revered.

'We will curse his name, challenge his power, and in our arrogance, we will march toward our inevitable doom. Shishupal and Dantavakra, the cousins who will not see beyond their hatred, will fall at the hands of Krishna. It is in this final incarnation, with bitter fury coursing through our veins, that we will meet our deaths. Yet, as we are struck down, there will be an escape from our cursed fate. In that moment, as my life bleeds out, I will merge once more into the essence of my beloved Vishnu, and the ancient curse of the Sanatkumaras will be lifted at last.

'This is the price we must pay for our hubris, for in each life I have sought to defy the divine, only to be reminded of my own insignificance. From Hiranyakashyapa to Ravana, and soon to be Shishupal—each life, a step closer to the inevitable. And yet, with every fall, I crawl toward the long-awaited union with the divine, a union I have resisted with every mortal breath but am now fated to embrace.'

—Ravana, Emperor of Lanka

NINE

Vengeful Cousins

A Double-edged Prophecy

The lands of Chedi and Karusha lay under the deep hues of *godhuli*, bathed in the light of a sinking sun that painted the rolling hills and river valleys in hues of flame and blood. The world seemed poised on the edge of change, as if nature itself anticipated the violent times to come. In these kingdoms, two figures would rise, whose destinies were intertwined by birth and prophecy, driven by ambition and hatred for a bitter rival—Krishna, the prince of Dwarka.

The tale begins with the strange birth of Shishupal. In the kingdom of Chedi, a great festival had been announced. King Damaghosha and his queen, Shrutashrava, awaited the birth of their firstborn, the long-anticipated heir to the Chedi throne. The royal lineage of Chedi, tracing its roots to the illustrious Yadava clan, was a symbol of strength, diplomacy, and nobility. But as the kingdom readied itself for celebration, an event of great foreboding unfolded in the royal chamber.

The baby was born under an unusual conjunction of planets, a celestial sign that had wise men muttering among themselves. When the child was finally revealed to his parents, a shroud of silence descended upon the room. The infant, though healthy and breathing, had three eyes and four arms. His countenance was unnatural—his third eye glowing with a disturbing gleam, and his two extra arms dangling grotesquely from his sides.

His first cries were not the innocent wails of a newborn, but the harsh braying of an ass—a sound that sent shivers through the hearts of those who heard it.

Shrutashrava and King Damaghosha, his father, stood frozen in horror as the child's misshapen body convulsed on the marble floor of the palace birthing chamber.

'Perhaps we should…' the king began, his voice shaking, but he was interrupted by a sudden, otherworldly presence. A deep voice, calm yet filled with authority, echoed in the chamber. It seemed to emanate from the very walls, as though the heavens had opened to deliver a message directly to those in attendance.

'Do not abandon this child,' the celestial voice commanded. 'He will grow to be strong and fortunate, a force that no mortal may easily defy. Yet, know this: his fate is sealed. He will fall by the hands of one already born, one whose mere touch shall strip him of his deformities. The one destined to slay him will be recognised when his additional eye and arms vanish.'

The king and queen exchanged glances, their fears tempered by curiosity and hope. Shrutashrava, clutching the child to her chest, asked with trembling lips, 'Who is this slayer of my son?'

The voice responded, 'The one you seek will reveal himself when you place the child on his lap. His extra limbs will fall away, and his unnatural eye will close, marking him as the harbinger of your son's end.'

Whispers spread through the halls like wildfire, and in the town below, superstitions flared. 'A demon is born,' they murmured, fear palpable in their voices.

The proclamation spread far and wide, carried on the wings of rumour across kingdoms and courts. Monarchs, eager to avoid becoming the prophesied slayer of such an ominous child, visited the palace, each holding the infant Shishupal on their laps. But none caused the child's deformities to fade. As time passed, the prophecy seemed to grow distant, nothing more than a whisper, and the people of Chedi started becoming accustomed to their strange prince.

During this time, the infant's cousin, the much-celebrated Krishna, visited the Chedi court. The grand halls of Chedi's palace were filled with the soft glow of flickering lamps, their light casting long shadows across the polished stone floors. The air was thick with the scent of incense, sweet and heady, swirling lazily as Krishna and Balarama entered the chamber, their presence commanding the attention of all who gathered there. Queen Shrutashrava, who was related to Krishna by blood, smiled warmly as she approached her nephews. Her heart swelled with pride at the sight of them.

'Welcome, Krishna. Welcome, Balarama,' the queen greeted them, her voice soft yet tinged with excitement. 'It is an honour to have you here.'

Krishna, ever serene, bowed his head in acknowledgment, his dark eyes gleaming with warmth. 'The honour is ours, dear aunt,' he said, his voice smooth as the flow of a river. 'I have heard much of the child. May I hold him?'

Shrutashrava hesitated, her fingers tightening around the bundle of silks cradling the infant. The parents had not thought to place Shishupal in Krishna's arms. After all, Krishna was much younger than many of the great kings and sages who had held her son before. The memory of the prophecy weighed heavily upon her heart, but the gentleness in Krishna's gaze soothed her fears. With a quiet nod, she stepped forward, her hands trembling slightly as she passed the child into Krishna's arms.

'As you wish,' she murmured, her breath shallow with a mixture of anticipation and anxiety.

Krishna took the child into his lap, his touch gentle and sure. For a moment, the room seemed to become still, as though the very air had paused in reverence. The flickering lamps grew dim, and an almost imperceptible shift occurred in the atmosphere.

As the child lay nestled in Krishna's arms, a sudden, subtle change swept over his form. The unnatural third eye, once glaring from the centre of his brow, slowly fluttered shut and vanished as if it had never been there. At the same time, the two extra arms, which had clawed and flailed since the boy's birth, withered and fell away, leaving Shishupal with the appearance of an ordinary child. A collective gasp rose from the onlookers, their eyes wide with astonishment. Yet, in the minds of Damaghosha and Shrutashrava, a new fear took root.

Shrutashrava, watching intently, felt her heart clench. She remembered the words of the celestial voice, the prophecy that foretold this very moment, and her blood ran cold. The boy holding her son was the one destined to end his life. Swallowing her fear, she stepped forward, her voice trembling with desperation.

'O Krishna, my dear nephew,' she implored, her hands clasped together in supplication. 'You know what the prophecy says… but I beg of you, forgive him. Spare my son from the fate that awaits him.'

Krishna looked up at his aunt, his face calm and unreadable, though his eyes held a trace of sadness. Gently, he lifted the now-normal child from his lap and handed him back to his mother.

'O aunt,' Krishna began, his voice soft but firm, 'I shall forgive your son for up to one hundred offences. Only if he goes beyond this will I be forced to act.'

The queen's lips trembled as she held her son close, tears of gratitude mingling with the deep sorrow she felt at hearing the unchangeable truth. 'Thank you,' she whispered, though the weight of Krishna's words lingered heavy in the room, a shadow that could not be dispelled.

With that, the moment passed, but the unspoken tension between destiny and hope settled like a veil over the hearts of those who had witnessed it. Although Krishna had healed Shishupal, according to the prophecy, he would one day be the cause of the boy's death.

Across the fertile plains of Karusha, another child had been born around the same time. Dantavakra, son of Vriddhasharman, was a towering boy, broad and sturdy, with a strength that belied his years. He was the antithesis of Shishupal in form but mirrored him in temperament. Wild and ferocious even in his youth, Dantavakra took pleasure in dominating his peers, his ambition matched only by his loyalty to his cousin Shishupal, whom he regarded as a brother in spirit.

Dantavakra's early life in Karusha was marked by displays of physical strength and raw courage. While Shishupal grew up surrounded by whispers of an infallible destiny, Dantavakra's upbringing was more grounded in forging his own path. From the age of six, he trained with the best warriors of the kingdom, excelling in combat and strategy. His father, King Vriddhasharman, was proud of his son's prowess, often remarking that no prince of Karusha had ever shown such strength at such a young age.

Despite his formidable talents, Dantavakra harboured a dark, untameable temper. When slighted, even in the smallest way, his wrath would erupt like a violent storm. One incident in his youth exemplified this. While sparring with his cousins in the royal courtyard, Dantavakra was knocked down by a well-placed blow from an elder prince. Enraged, he leapt to his feet and, with terrifying strength, hurled the young man across the courtyard, breaking several of his ribs. The incident cemented Dantavakra's reputation not only as a warrior of promise but as a figure to be feared.

As he grew, his loyalty to Shishupal deepened. The two cousins, despite their differing backgrounds, found common ground in their shared ambition and mutual disdain for Krishna, the prince of Dwarka. While Shishupal was shrewd, cunning, and capable of manipulation through words, Dantavakra was fierce, impetuous, and driven by sheer force. Their time together was spent honing their skills in combat, statecraft, and strategy. Dantavakra's wild nature was tempered only by Shishupal's influence, and together, they forged a bond of brotherhood. In secret, they would speak of their desire for conquest, of kingdoms that would tremble at their feet, and of the one obstacle in their path—Krishna.

However, it was not only Krishna's prowess that gnawed at Shishupal. The prophecy that tied his fate to Krishna simmered beneath the surface, growing into a smouldering resentment.

In their youth, both Shishupal and Dantavakra found themselves drawn into the orbit of Jarasandha, the mighty king of Magadha. Jarasandha's name was synonymous with fear across the kingdoms of Aryavarta. His strength was unmatched, and his ambition knew no bounds. Shishupal and Dantavakra admired Jarasandha for his military prowess, and his ruthlessness.

In Jarasandha, the cousins found the guide they needed. The cousins sought Jarasandha's mentorship, and he accepted them. Under Jarasandha's tutelage, they honed their thirst for power and vengeance. Jarasandha, who shared their disdain for Krishna, nurtured their ambitions, teaching them the importance of alliances, subjugation, and the swift annihilation of those who stood in their way.

'You are both destined for greatness,' Jarasandha would tell them, his voice booming like thunder in the war halls of Magadha. 'But greatness is not earned through birthright alone. It must be taken by force, by cunning, and by blood. Krishna is a usurper—a mere herder who pretends to be a king. You, Shishupal, you are a true king, and it is your right to rule this land.'

Shishupal soaked in these words like dry earth soaking in rain. His disdain for Krishna grew, transforming into a personal vendetta. The prophecy that had haunted him since birth now fuelled his desire to defeat his cousin, not as an act of fate, but a deliberate, calculated decision.

As Shishupal and Dantavakra matured, their friendship with Jarasandha's children, especially his sons, further cemented their loyalty to the Magadha king. They became his most trusted allies in his campaigns against the Yadavas, lending their strength to his cause. Shishupal, with his keen intellect, often devised battle strategies, while Dantavakra led the charge on the battlefield with reckless abandon, carving a path of blood wherever he went.

But it was not enough. Krishna, the prince of Dwarka, remained untouchable, always one step ahead of them. The frustration ate at Shishupal, turning his mind towards darker thoughts. He knew that to truly stand against Krishna, he would need more than just brute strength and alliances.

Among their circle of companions was Rukmi, the prince of Vidarbha, whose charisma and cunning often set the tone for their conspiracies. He, too, despised Krishna, albeit for different reasons. Rukmi had always been envious of Krishna's valour and the tales of his prowess that reached every corner of the land. More importantly, he harboured a deep desire to marry off his sister, Rukmini, to Shishupal, cementing an alliance that would challenge the growing might of Dwarka.

The promise of marriage between Shishupal and Rukmini had been made long before the storm of wars and alliances ever darkened the horizon. Shishupal, though fierce and ambitious, had been captivated by Rukmini's grace and beauty from a young age. Rukmi, ever eager to solidify the bonds of power, had encouraged the match. He saw in Shishupal not only a future brother-in-law but a strong ally who could stand beside him against Krishna, whom he had always envied and feared.

'I will make Rukmini your bride,' Rukmi had promised, his voice confident as they sat one evening in the gardens of Vidarbha. The air was thick with the scent of jasmine, and the setting sun cast a crimson glow over the palace. 'And together, we will ensure that no kingdom dares challenge our might.'

Shishupal had smiled then, a rare, almost serene expression passing over his usually fierce face. 'With Rukmini by my side, I will have all that I desire. But first, there is the matter of Krishna. His shadow looms too large, even from Dwarka.'

At the time, none of them could have imagined how that shadow would grow, casting a pall over their grand ambitions.

'In the future, the cycle of the curse of the Sanatkumaras will continue and culminate in my rebirth as Shishupal, destined from birth to meet my end at the hands of Krishna. At my birth itself, it will be foretold that I would die at his hands, and yet, my arrogance and hatred towards him will grow. My insults and defiance will be unending, each act of disrespect a futile attempt to alter my destiny. In the court of Yudhishthira, my final confrontation will come. I will hurl invectives at Krishna, testing the limits of his patience. When his wrath finally manifests, the Sudarshana Chakra will cleave my head, fulfilling the prophecy.

'My life and death as Shishupal will be a testament to the inescapability of karma and the futility of resisting divine will. Let my future tale be a warning to all who harbour hatred and arrogance: the divine order is supreme, and resistance only brings inevitable doom. Embrace humility, for it is in understanding and accepting one's fate that true peace is found.'

–Ravana, Emperor of Lanka

TEN

The Abduction of Rukmini

Envy Is a One-Way Street

News of Kansa's death reached the courts of Chedi and Karusha. It shook the teenage cousins to their core. Kansa had been a titan, feared even by the gods, and now he was no more, struck down by his nephew.

Shishupal stood at the head of a grand banquet in his father's hall when a breathless messenger burst through the doors. 'My lord! Kansa of Mathura is dead!'

The words hung in the air like a curse, freezing the celebration into silence. Shishupal's goblet slipped from his hand, crashing to the floor, forgotten. 'Who dares?' His voice, a low growl, quivered with disbelief.

'It was Krishna,' the messenger said, bowing his head as if to shield himself from Shishupal's rage. 'The Yadava prince has slain him in single combat.'

Shishupal's face twisted into a mask of fury, his arms clenching tightly into fists. 'Krishna again,' he spat, his voice heavy with contempt. 'What manner of treachery is this? How could Kansa fall to a mere shepherd?'

Dantavakra, who had been reclining against a pillar, rose to his feet, his towering frame casting a shadow over the chamber. 'This cannot go unanswered,' he declared. 'Jarasandha will demand vengeance, and we will stand with him. We shall see if Krishna's luck holds against true warriors.'

Shishupal nodded, his face darkening further. His hatred for Krishna had always simmered beneath the surface, but now it flared into a consuming fire. He could already see the path before him—one that led to bloodshed and war. Shishupal's eyes narrowed. 'It is not just Kansa's death. Jarasandha's daughters are now widows. The great king of Magadha will not let this stand.'

It was not long before Shishupal, Dantavakra, and Rukmi made their way to Magadha. They stood together before Jarasandha, their faces set in grim determination. The king of Magadha regarded them with approval. These were not the hesitant monarchs of other realms, bound by the fear of Krishna's growing legend. These were warriors, eager for battle, their hearts filled with hatred.

'Together,' Jarasandha said, his voice filling the great hall of Magadha's palace, 'we will make the earth tremble. We will wipe Dwarka from the face of Bharatavarsha. And Krishna... Krishna will know the true meaning of suffering.'

Shishupal, whose eyes burned with a mad fury, stepped forward. 'My lord,' he said, bowing deeply, 'let me lead the charge. Let me strike the first blow against this... usurper.'

Jarasandha smiled, a cold and merciless grin. 'You shall have your chance, Shishupal. But be warned—Krishna is no ordinary foe. We must strike with all our might, and even then, victory is not certain.'

Shishupal, his fiery eyes matching the intensity of the king's, spoke with conviction. 'I will tear down the walls of Mathura and crush this upstart.'

A campaign of terror began, with Jarasandha leading seventeen attacks on Mathura. Each time, Krishna and Balarama stood firm, their forces smaller in number but bolstered by strategy and the sheer will of their leaders. The city's defences were legendary, and the Yadavas repelled each attack Jarasandha launched with relentless courage.

But as the years wore on, Krishna realised that Mathura could not withstand the repeated assaults forever. With great care, he orchestrated an escape, a retreat that would be recounted as legend for generations. Under the cover of darkness, while Jarasandha prepared for yet another siege, the entire Yadava clan slipped away silently, making their way to the distant shores of the western sea. There, they would build a new fortress, a city that would stand as a testament to their resilience—Dwarka.

When Jarasandha's forces finally broke through the gates of Mathura, they found nothing but an empty city, its halls deserted and its streets eerily silent. The fury of the king of Magadha knew no bounds, but there was nothing left to conquer.

Shishupal and Dantavakra stood amidst the hollow ruins, their hearts heavy with frustration and rage. This escape had robbed them of their vengeance, but it had not crushed their ambition.

In the aftermath of this long war, Rukmi turned to his friend, oblivious to the storm that awaited them in the future. 'The war is behind us now, my friend. And as I promised, my sister Rukmini will be your wife.'

Shishupal nodded, his mind already turning to thoughts of power, conquest, and the final reckoning with the one man who had eluded him for so long. The shadow of Krishna still lingered, but now, with Rukmini's hand, Shishupal believed he could finally begin to shape his destiny.

Little did he know, the threads of fate were still being woven, and the storm that would change everything was only just beginning to gather strength.

The golden sun hung low in the sky, casting long shadows over the opulent halls of the Chedi palace. Shishupal paced restlessly across the glittering stone floors beneath his feet, casting reflections of his dark mood. The courtiers were celebrating, drinking from cups of polished silver, their laughter echoing through the corridors. They were already speaking of him as 'the fortunate groom,' the man who would wed the most beautiful woman in Aryavarta, Rukmini, the princess of Vidarbha. But behind Shishupal's hard eyes, something darker was brewing.

His thoughts drifted to Rukmini, the woman destined to become his queen. He did not love Rukmini—no, that was too soft a word for a man like him—but the thought of possessing her filled him with a triumphant satisfaction. She was to be his bride, a prize that would elevate him further into the heights of power. With her by his side, he would gain influence over Vidarbha and strengthen his alliances with men like Jarasandha, his mentor and guide. The marriage was as much about the conquest of land and prestige as it was about the dominion over a beautiful woman.

But in the depths of his heart, Shishupal felt a gnawing uncertainty. Rukmini was not merely a piece on his chessboard; she had a mind of her own, a spirit that defied possession. He could not shake the feeling that something did not seem right.

Despite the assurances from Rukmi, her brother and his close friend, a gnawing doubt haunted him. He had heard rumours—whispers of Krishna, that arrogant prince of Dwarka. Shishupal's lip curled in disdain at the memory. Kansa, the rightful king of Mathura, had been struck down by this upstart. His blood still boiled when he thought of it. But what enraged him more was that Krishna had been spoken of in connection to Rukmini. It was no secret that she admired him, that her heart, traitorous and foolish, leaned toward the one man Shishupal despised above all.

Shishupal halted in his pacing, his fingers flexing at his side as though they ached to grasp the hilt of his sword. He had vowed to bring Krishna down—ever since the insult of Kansa's death, he had waited for the moment to crush him, to make him suffer. And now, that moment was within his grasp.

Jarasandha had assured him that the time would come when Krishna's growing influence would be checked. But first, he needed to secure his bride, to cement his power through the union with Rukmini. Then, and only then, would he deal with Krishna.

Rukmini stood alone in her chambers, gazing out of her window at the sprawling city below, her heart heavy. Dressed in the finest silks, her dark hair braided with jasmine flowers, she should have been the picture of a radiant bride. But her face, pale and drawn, betrayed the turmoil roiling inside her. She felt like a prisoner in the most luxurious of cages.

The man she was to marry tomorrow was not a man of honour. Shishupal, the prince of Chedi, had proven time and again that cruelty ran in his blood. His haughty laughter echoed in her ears as she recalled how, on his visits to Vidarbha, he boasted about his conquests in war and the terror he sowed in villages. His eyes gleamed when he recounted stories of prisoners being tortured, of cities burnt to the ground. There was no nobility in him, no compassion.

But worse than his cruelty was his arrogance. Shishupal believed that power gave him the right to take whatever he desired. Rukmini was simply the latest prize, a queen to sit beside him as he trampled over kingdoms. The thought of binding herself to such a man sickened her.

Her only solace was in the secret letter she had sent days ago. A letter written with trembling hands and a heart full of hope. A letter to Krishna, the one man she had never met but whose very name filled her heart with longing.

She had heard of him, of course. Every kingdom had. Krishna, the prince of Dwarka, the man who had killed the tyrant Kansa and restored justice to the lands of Mathura. His wisdom and strength were legendary, and his mere presence commanded respect. But more than the stories of his might, it was his character that had captured Rukmini's heart. His kindness, his fairness—qualities that stood in stark contrast to the darkness of Shishupal.

In her letter, Rukmini had poured out her soul:

'Come, O Krishna, and take me as your own. Save me from this dreadful fate, for I would rather die than live as Shishupal's queen.'

Her heart raced each time she thought of her letter. Would Krishna come? Had he received it? Or was she doomed to the fate her brother Rukmi had sealed for her? For Rukmi, Vidarbha's prince, had made no secret of his admiration for Shishupal. The two men, united by ambition and lust for power, had decided to arrange this match without once taking her wishes into consideration.

The sun was setting now, casting a golden glow over the city, but in Rukmini's heart, all was shadow.

The day of the wedding dawned with fanfare. Rukmini was led through the palace, where nobles from across the land gathered to witness her marriage to Shishupal. Dressed in red silks, her face veiled, she moved through the celebrations as if in a trance. But beneath her composed exterior, her heart was racing.

By tradition, the bride was to visit the temple of

Parvati, just beyond the city walls, to offer her prayers before the wedding. This was her moment. If Krishna was coming, this was where he would find her.

As she knelt before the idol of the goddess, her hands clasped in prayer, her heart pounded in her chest. The priests chanted sacred mantras, the air heavy with the scent of sandalwood and flowers, but Rukmini could barely hear them over the sound of her own thoughts. *Would Krishna come?*

She opened her eyes and stood, moving to the temple's threshold. The wide plains stretched out before her, and beyond them lay freedom or despair. Her breath caught in her throat. There, in the distance, a figure appeared, riding fast in a golden chariot. Her heart leapt.

Krishna had come.

The chariot raced across the fields, a blur of speed and grace, as Krishna guided the horses with unmatched skill. His dark form gleamed under the sunlight, and as he drew closer, Rukmini could see the calm determination in his eyes. He wore a golden crown that sparkled in the light, and his chariot was like none she had ever seen—majestic, as if crafted by the gods themselves.

He rode straight toward her, and without hesitation, extended his hand.

'Come,' he said, his voice soft yet firm. 'We must leave before it's too late.'

Rukmini did not hesitate. With one swift movement, she took Krishna's hand and stepped into the chariot. Her heart pounded with a mix of fear and exhilaration.

Krishna, the man she had admired from afar, was now her rescuer. As soon as she was inside the chariot, Krishna lashed the reins, and the horses surged forward, speeding away from the temple.

The celebration inside the palace quickly turned to confusion and outrage when the news of Rukmini's abduction reached the gathered guests. Shishupal, dressed in his wedding finery, turned pale with fury as the messenger stammered out the details of the princess's escape.

Shishupal's breath stopped for a moment, his vision turning red. The world around him blurred as rage boiled up from within, a burning hatred so fierce he could barely contain it. 'Krishna,' he spat, the name a curse on his lips. 'That coward!'

His fury erupted in a roar that echoed through the palace halls. The courtiers who had been preparing for the wedding now looked on in terror as Shishupal's wrath consumed him. He slammed his fist into a nearby pillar, cracking the marble under his sheer strength.

'I will kill him!' he bellowed. 'I will cut him down where he stands and drag his body through the streets like a common criminal!'

Shishupal stormed through the palace, gathering his forces. Rukmi, equally humiliated, rushed to join him, though the fear in his eyes betrayed his uncertainty. The Vidarbha prince had made a grave error in underestimating Krishna, and now, both he and Shishupal were paying the price for their arrogance.

'We ride at once,' Rukmi declared, his eyes blazing with anger. 'Krishna will not escape. He will pay for this with his life.'

In a matter of minutes, Shishupal and Rukmi had gathered a vast army. Warriors mounted their horses and chariots, their swords and spears gleaming under the midday sun, and rode out from the gates of Vidarbha in hot pursuit of Krishna's chariot. The air was filled with the thunder of hooves and the clatter of armour as the army sped across the plains, determined to reclaim their lost prize.

As he raced in his chariot, fury coursing through his veins like fire, Shishupal felt the power of his position surge within him. He would not be made a fool of again. The soldiers of Chedi rallied around him, their loyalty unwavering. They shared his hatred for Krishna and knew that this was more than a fight for Rukmini; it was a fight for honour.

The chariot raced through the streets of Chedi, the horses galloping as if sensing their master's rage. Shishupal's mind was a tempest, swirling with thoughts of retribution. He could envision Rukmini's face as Krishna spirited her away, her expression one of shock and despair. The thought twisted his heart into knots.

'Where is he?' Shishupal shouted to his men, his voice hoarse with fury. 'Where are Krishna and Rukmini?'

The soldiers pointed toward the distance, where a plume of dust rose in the air. 'That way, my lord!'

With renewed fervour, Shishupal urged his horses faster, the wind whipping against his face as they tore through the landscape. He could see it now, the distant outline of Krishna's chariot racing ahead, a dark silhouette against the setting sun. Rage blinded him as he pushed his horses to their limits.

'Faster! We will not let him escape!'

The chase continued, and soon they entered the vast plains that stretched between Chedi and Dwarka. Shishupal could see Krishna's chariot ahead amidst the glow of the setting sun, the figure of the prince standing tall and defiant, with Rukmini beside him. The sight sent a wave of humiliation crashing over him.

As they drew closer, Krishna could see the cloud of dust rising from the horizon, signalling the approach of Shishupal's forces. Rukmini, seated beside him in the chariot, glanced nervously at the oncoming army.

'They will catch us,' she whispered, fear lacing her voice.

Krishna, however, remained calm. He guided the horses with expert precision, their speed unmatched by the warriors who chased them. 'Do not fear,' he said, his voice soothing yet firm. 'They will not catch us.'

ELEVEN

The Fall of Shishupal

Impotent Rage

Shishupal's frustration grew with every passing moment. As they closed the gap, Shishupal caught sight of Krishna's calm face, untouched by the chaos around him. It was as if the battlefield meant nothing to him. Shishupal's fury reached a fever pitch. How dare he, this common cowherd, this upstart, look upon him with such disdain?

Shishupal raced towards the lone chariot with unrelenting fury. 'You will pay for this, you coward,' he shouted, raising his sword high into the air. 'I will slay you right here!' His voice was raw with anger. 'Face me and accept your fate!'

'Why would I waste my time on you when there are far greater challenges to confront?' Krishna replied, a mocking tone lacing his words. 'But if it is a duel you seek, then so be it.'

The two chariots collided, and Shishupal leapt from his chariot, closing the distance between them. The sound of metal clashing filled the air as their swords met. Shishupal felt the rush of adrenaline as he pushed against Krishna's strength, their blades locked in a battle of wills. 'I will not let you take her!' he spat, his eyes blazing with fury.

'Why not?' Krishna replied, effortlessly pushing Shishupal back. 'She does not belong to you. She has chosen her path, and you cannot force her to do your bidding.'

With a primal roar, Shishupal swung his sword, aiming for Krishna's neck, but Krishna ducked, moving with the grace of a gazelle. The two danced in a deadly rhythm, each strike met with a counter, each moment charged with the tension of their animosity.

As the clash continued, the sun dipped below the horizon, casting an eerie light upon the battlefield. Shishupal felt weariness creep into his limbs, but the fire of his hatred kept him going. With a final surge of strength, he lunged forward, bringing his sword down with all his might. Krishna sidestepped, his movements fluid and effortless.

'Is this all you have, Shishupal?' Krishna taunted, dodging another strike. 'Your rage blinds you to the truth.'

'I am done with your games!' Shishupal roared, the frustration boiling within him. 'You consider yourself a god, but you are nothing but a mere thief!'

With renewed fury, Shishupal unleashed a series of attacks, his movements fuelled by desperation. Each swing of his sword grew more ferocious, more erratic, but Krishna remained unfazed, his smile ever-present.

'Let go of your anger, Shishupal. It will only lead to your downfall,' Krishna advised, his voice calm as the storm raged around them.

The words struck like a hammer on the anvil of Shishupal's mind. The realisation hit him like a tidal wave. He was losing, and the bitter truth gnawed at his insides.

'Enough!' Shishupal shouted, gathering his strength for one final blow. But as he swung his sword, Krishna moved with such speed that it was as if he had vanished, reappearing behind Shishupal.

In one swift motion, Krishna disarmed Shishupal, sending the sword flying from his grasp. 'It seems your rage has left you vulnerable,' he said, the smirk still dancing on his lips.

Shishupal turned, eyes blazing with fury, but it was too late. Krishna moved with a fluidity that seemed almost magical, delivering a blow that sent Shishupal sprawling to the ground. The world around him spun as he tried to regain his footing, but the realisation of defeat settled heavily in his chest.

'You see, Shishupal, strength alone does not determine the outcome of a battle,' Krishna said, standing tall over his fallen adversary. 'It is strategy, intelligence, and the heart that truly matter.'

Shishupal's spirit seemed to wane, the weight of his failures crashing down upon him. 'Krishna!' he spat, rage and humiliation mingling in his voice. 'You will pay for this! I will not let you take her!'

Krishna's expression shifted slightly, a glimmer of pity crossing his features. 'She is not a trophy to be won, Shishupal. If you truly loved her, you would let her choose her own fate.'

Shishupal's fury boiled over, his hatred festering like

a poison in his soul. He had failed. Krishna had taken everything from him—his bride, his pride, and now his honour. The Chedi prince staggered to his feet, glaring at the man who had humiliated him.

But Krishna had no more interest in the battle. He turned away, leading Rukmini to his chariot.

Shishupal watched as they rode away, his heart blackened by his impotence, by the realisation that Krishna had defeated him without ever truly trying. His hatred grew, a smouldering fire that would never be extinguished. He would have his revenge, no matter the cost.

In the days that followed, the bitter taste of humiliation lingered in Shishupal's mouth like ash. The walls of his palace felt constricting, a prison of his own making. He had lost not only Rukmini but also his chance to claim supremacy over Krishna. Each passing hour fuelled his hatred, igniting the flames of vengeance that threatened to consume him whole.

Days turned into weeks as Shishupal strategised his revenge. He could not forget the sight of Rukmini riding away with Krishna, the mocking smile on Krishna's face forever etched in his memory. It became a twisted mantra in his mind—a vow that he would stop at nothing to exact his revenge.

Shishupal's gaze often turned toward the kingdom of Magadha, where Jarasandha ruled. The thought of enlisting his aid became an obsession, for he knew that Jarasandha harboured his own grievances against Krishna.

The day finally arrived when Shishupal set out to meet Jarasandha. As he entered the grand halls of Magadha, the atmosphere was thick with tension. The powerful king of Magadha was a formidable ally, and Shishupal knew he had to tread carefully.

'Welcome, Shishupal,' Jarasandha said, his voice deep and resonant. 'What brings you to my kingdom?'

'I seek your alliance against Krishna,' Shishupal stated boldly, his eyes meeting Jarasandha's. 'He has humiliated me, and I know he has also wronged you.'

Jarasandha leaned back on his throne, studying Shishupal with keen interest. 'You wish to unite our forces against the prince of Dwarka? What do you propose?'

'A great army,' Shishupal replied, excitement creeping into his voice. 'We will strike when he least expects it, crush him before he can react!'

The two men discussed strategies late into the night, their voices echoing through the grand halls of the palace. Shishupal felt a flicker of hope igniting within him. With Jarasandha by his side, they could turn the tide against Krishna once and for all.

But fate, it seemed, had its own designs. News of a great duel between Jarasandha and Bhima of the Pandavas reached Shishupal. The anticipation of victory turned to dread as the whispers of Bhima's strength echoed through the halls. He knew Krishna had a hand in this, guiding the Pandavas, and the thought drove him to the brink of madness.

As the duel commenced, Shishupal watched from a

distance, his heart pounding in his chest. Jarasandha, strong and resolute, faced Bhima with a fierce intensity. But as the two titans clashed, the realisation hit Shishupal that Jarasandha was getting old and hardly a match for the far younger Bhima. Why had he agreed to this mismatched duel?

Bhima was relentless, the raw power behind each strike unyielding. With every blow, Shishupal felt his hope waning. Jarasandha fought valiantly, but Bhima's resolve was like a tide, overwhelming and unstoppable.

'Come on, O mighty Jarasandha!' Shishupal shouted, frustration bubbling over. 'You cannot lose! Not now!'

But fate had other plans. With a final, decisive blow, Bhima unleashed his strength, and tore Jarasandha apart. The roar of victory echoed across the battlefield. Shishupal felt the world tilt beneath him as he witnessed Jarasandha's fall.

'No!' he bellowed, his voice filled with impotent rage. 'This cannot be!'

As the dust settled, Shishupal's dreams lay in ruins, scattered like ashes in the wind. The realisation that he had lost not only Rukmini but also a powerful ally drove him into the depths of despair. The laughter of his enemies echoed in his mind, mocking him, reminding him of his failures.

Shishupal wept hot tears of rage.

The death of Jarasandha sent shockwaves through the kingdoms of Aryavarta. Shishupal felt a rising dread in his chest. Jarasandha's death would mean the fall of

Magadha, the crumbling of his strongest ally. Without Jarasandha, who would stand against Krishna's growing power? Who would fight against the man who had stolen everything from him?

With Jarasandha dead, Krishna stood taller than ever before, his power and influence unrivalled in Aryavarta. But as Krishna returned to Dwarka, victorious once again, Shishupal's heart was consumed by a single, burning desire: Vengeance.

Many years passed.

Shishupal, now matured into a hardened king of Chedi, sat amidst his court, cloaked in the trappings of power and vengeance. His face, sharp and angular, was a mask of bitterness that time had only deepened. The weight of years of hatred, festering like an open wound, had carved deep lines into his features. His fingers tapped restlessly on the arm of his throne, an outward sign of the inner turmoil that was ever-present.

The news had come a few days prior: the Pandava king, Yudhishthira, had invited all the lords and rulers of the land to Hastinapur to witness the grand *Rajasuya Yajna*, symbolising his undisputed claim over the throne of Bharatavarsha.

As was the custom, the first honour—*Arghya*, or the 'offering of the first respect'—would be given to one among the assembled lords, marking them as the highest in esteem.

The great hall of Hastinapur was a spectacle of magnificence. The air was thick with the fragrance of flowers and incense, and the chatter of lords and dignitaries echoed off the walls. As the guests arrived, the atmosphere buzzed with excitement and anticipation. Kings and warriors from across Bharatavarsha filled the hall, their colourful attire contrasting against the ornate golden decorations.

Shishupal's royal chariot, drawn by powerful steeds, rolled through the entrance, the banners of Chedi fluttering ominously in the breeze.

With a deep breath, Shishupal stepped down from his chariot, his armour gleaming like the sharp edge of a dagger. His eyes scanned the hall, taking in the sight of the assembled kings. But it was the presence of Krishna, seated near Yudhishthira, that ignited a fire within him. The mere sight of the Yadava prince made his blood boil, a potent reminder of the humiliations he had suffered at Krishna's hands.

As Shishupal strode into the hall, he felt the weight of every gaze upon him, but he remained undeterred. He approached Yudhishthira, a mask of forced civility overlaid with smouldering anger. 'Cousin,' he greeted, his voice steady but laced with contempt. 'I come in honour of this great occasion.'

Yudhishthira, always the diplomat, offered a warm smile. 'We are grateful for your presence, Shishupal. Together, we shall celebrate this day.'

Just then, Sahadeva stepped forward, 'The first

honour, *Arghya*, shall be offered to Krishna of Dwarka, who stands above all in wisdom, power, and virtue.'

A murmur rippled through the hall, but it was quickly silenced by the respect Krishna commanded. Yet, one man stood unmoved by the reverence in the air. Shishupal rose from his seat, his face twisted in contempt.

'I protest!' His voice rang out, sharp and cutting, drawing the eyes of every king in the hall. 'This insult I cannot stand. How can we, the lords of Aryavarta, bow our heads to a mere cowherd? A thief who has stolen kingdoms, wives, and honour from those more deserving!'

The hall fell into shocked silence. No one had ever dared speak of Krishna in such a manner, least of all in the presence of the assembled royalty. Krishna's expression remained calm, though a shadow passed over his features. Yudhishthira, sensing the tension, tried to intervene.

'Shishupal,' Yudhishthira said diplomatically, 'let us not mar this occasion with anger. The honour has been rightfully given. Krishna is deserving of our respect.'

But Shishupal would not be placated. 'Rightfully given?' he scoffed. 'This man is a serpent, a deceiver, who hides behind words of peace while spreading chaos. He betrayed his own kin, sided with the enemies of his people, and now, like a jackal, he seeks to claim what is not his.'

Krishna stood, his gaze steady. 'Shishupal, you have spoken enough. This is not the time or place for such accusations.'

Shishupal's rage flared. 'Enough? No, Krishna. I will not be silenced by you. You claim to be a protector, a friend of righteousness, but you are nothing more than a coward who hides behind others to do your bidding. You ran from battle in Mathura, you abandoned your people, and you have the audacity to sit here and demand respect?'

The kings around them shifted uncomfortably, but none dared to speak. Shishupal's insults had crossed into dangerous territory, but Krishna remained unruffled. He raised his hand, signalling for silence.

'I have spared you many times, Shishupal,' Krishna said, his voice calm but carrying the weight of an impending storm. 'Your mother once asked me for mercy, and I granted it. I promised to forgive one hundred offences, but you have tested my patience long enough.'

Shishupal sneered. 'Spare me your sanctimony, Krishna. I will not bow to a man who hides behind divine favour.'

Krishna's eyes darkened. 'This is your final warning. You have reached the limit of your offences.'

The hall was tense with anticipation. The air crackled with the energy of impending violence. Shishupal, blinded by his rage and bitterness, stepped forward, his hand on the hilt of his sword.

The memory of his youth returned to him, of the day Krishna had held him as a baby, and his extra limbs had fallen away—a mark of fate, as the sages had said, that Krishna would one day be his doom. His mother had begged Krishna for mercy, and Krishna, with his characteristic arrogance, had agreed to spare his life—on one condition. Shishupal would be forgiven one hundred offences. One hundred slights, insults, or attacks, and no more. Krishna's words had haunted him ever since.

'One hundred,' Shishupal muttered, gripping the hilt of his sword as if it would offer him some solace.

'Strike me down if you dare, Krishna! Show all these kings your true nature—a tyrant who cannot bear to be challenged!'

The words hung in the air for a moment, and then, like the breaking of a dam, the tension snapped. Krishna, moving with a speed that seemed otherworldly, raised his hand. The legendary *Sudarshana Chakra*, the divine discus that had felled countless enemies, materialised in his palm. The kings gasped as the weapon spun, its edges gleaming with deadly light.

Shishupal barely had time to react. With a single, swift motion, Krishna released the chakra. It sliced through the air, a blur of light and power, and before anyone could even draw breath, it found its mark.

The sound of the impact was like thunder, a deafening crack that reverberated through the hall. Shishupal stood frozen, his eyes wide with disbelief. For a moment, he remained standing, as if his body had not yet realised what had happened. Then, slowly, almost gracefully, he crumpled to the ground. The chakra had cleaved his head from his body, ending his life in an instant.

The hall was silent, save for the soft hum of the chakra as it returned to Krishna's hand. Shishupal's lifeless body lay at the feet of the assembly, his years of rage and hatred extinguished in a single stroke.

Krishna looked down at the fallen king, his expression

unreadable. 'I warned you,' he said softly, almost as if speaking to himself. 'One hundred offences. No more.'

The kings of Aryavarta, who had witnessed countless battles and wars, sat in stunned silence. Even the great warriors among them—men like Bhishma, Karna, and Drona—were humbled by the display of power. Shishupal had been a king of great renown, but in the end, his hatred had led him to his doom.

Yudhishthira, shaken by the violence but bound by duty, stood and addressed the assembly. 'The Rajasuya Yajna has commenced and it will not be stopped now. Let us honour Shishupal's spirit and continue with the ceremony. Any monarch who wishes to leave, is welcome to do so.'

No king moved, as Shishupal's decapitated body was removed and the hall sanctified with holy chants. With all due respect, Yudhishthira offered *Arghya* to Krishna amidst holy chants.

The *Rajasuya Yajna* continued amidst an atmosphere heavy with reflection and sorrow. Shishupal's legacy would be one of caution, a reminder of the thin line between honour and disgrace, power and folly.

'In his final mortal incarnation, my brother Vijaya will be reborn as Dantavakra, bound by destiny to oppose the divine once more. As a friend and ally of Shishupal, his loyalty will lead him to confront Krishna, seeking revenge for his fallen comrade. His heart will be filled with rage and defiance, his mind clouded by the desire for retribution. In his final battle, he will face Krishna, the avatar of Vishnu, knowing well the prophecy that foretold his demise.

'Despite his strength and fury, he will be no match for the divine. With a single blow from his mace, Krishna will end his life, completing the cycle of the curse that began with our arrogance as Jaya and Vijaya. His fall as Dantavakra will be a reminder that loyalty, when misguided, can lead to destruction.

'The cosmic order prevails, and resistance against it is futile. Let Dantavakra's story serve as a lesson: true loyalty is to the divine order, and embracing one's fate with humility is the path to redemption. In his end, see the wisdom of accepting the divine will, for it is in surrender that one finds true liberation.'

–Ravana, Emperor of Lanka

TWELVE

The Reckoning of Dantavakra

Doorway to Foolhardiness

The sky above was clear, a deep blue unblemished by clouds, but the air itself carried the weight of an impending storm. The ground trembled underfoot as Dantavakra strode forward, his massive frame dwarfing the landscape. His crooked teeth, the feature that had given him his name, clenched tightly in a grimace of fury. Dantavakra, the king of Karusha, was a man driven by vengeance, consumed by the desire to avenge the death of his closest friend Shishupal, slain by Krishna at the Rajasuya Yagya.

He could still recall the day his parents had named him after his teeth had grown crooked, giving him a fierce and fearsome appearance even as a child. Vriddhasharman, his father, had always been proud of his son's strength, while Shrutadeva, his mother—Kunti's sister—had often spoken of their illustrious family ties. Yet that shared blood with Krishna was now a bitter memory. Their kinship meant nothing to him, not after all that had transpired.

He had refused to attend the Rajasuya Yagya in protest after hearing of the death of Jarasandha, and now, after hearing that Krishna was on his way to Dwaraka, fresh from his victories, Dantavakra's rage had reached its boiling point. Today, it would all end—one way or another.

The world blurred around him, the colours fading into a haze of red as he marched forward, his anger fuelling his every stride. The battleground was only a little distance away now, and the thought of confronting his rival filled him with both dread and exhilaration. The air grew heavier with each step, laden with the promise of confrontation.

The wind picked up as Dantavakra neared the place where he would confront his enemy. His fury was palpable, a physical force that seemed to bend the air around him. He had come without armour, without a chariot, and without any of the tools of war, save for his club. His anger alone was his weapon, burning fiercer than any fire.

His footsteps were thunderous, each one sending vibrations through the earth as he walked. With every step he took, memories surged through him: Shishupal's laughter, their shared dreams of power, and the bitter realisation of betrayal. The visions of their past together twisted in his mind like a storm, growing darker with the memory of Krishna's taunts and his reckless victories. The air crackled with anticipation, as if nature itself sensed the brewing storm within him.

Dantavakra's heart raced as he recalled the moment that had driven him to this furious brink: the day

Krishna had killed Salva, the king of Kashi, a man whom Dantavakra held in high regard. The loss of Shishupal had been a personal blow, but Salva's death had ignited a fire within him, a call to arms that he could not ignore. It was in the heat of that moment, amidst the whispers of vengeance swirling around him, that he had taken the solemn vow to avenge his friends.

'He will come,' Dantavakra growled to himself, gripping his club so tightly that his knuckles turned white. 'Krishna will not escape me today.'

As if summoned by his thoughts, a figure appeared in the distance, the unmistakable form of Krishna seated in his gleaming chariot. His posture was relaxed, his demeanour calm, but there was a sharpness in his eyes, a readiness that did not escape Dantavakra's notice. The sight of his cousin, the slayer of his friends, stoked the fires of his hatred even further.

'Krishna!' Dantavakra bellowed, his voice shaking the very heavens. 'You coward! Come face me, if you dare! You have killed my friends—first Jarasandha, then Shishupal—and now you seek to flee to Dwaraka? Face me, and we will settle this, once and for all.'

Krishna's chariot slowed to a halt, and with a grace that seemed almost otherworldly, he stepped down from it, holding his *Kaumodaki* club. Krishna's expression was unreadable, his gaze steady as he regarded the towering figure of Dantavakra.

'Dantavakra,' Krishna called out, his voice calm but carrying easily over the distance between them, 'you are driven by rage, by vengeance. You seek to fight me for the deaths of your friends, but their choices brought them to their end. Do not let this blind fury lead you to the same fate.'

Dantavakra sneered, his crooked teeth bared in a snarl. 'Spare me your words, Krishna! You think yourself a hero, but you are nothing more than a murderer, hiding behind false wisdom. You took Shishupal from me, and now, you wish to take me as well!' He raised his club high, the veins in his arms bulging with the strain. 'But I will not be as easy to kill as they were.'

Krishna said nothing in response, only readied himself, gripping his club firmly. There was a moment of stillness, as if the entire world held its breath, waiting for the inevitable clash. And then, with a roar that could have split the heavens, Dantavakra charged, his massive feet pounding the earth as he rushed toward Krishna, his club raised high.

The ground seemed to tremble beneath him as he advanced, his muscles straining with every step. He swung his club down toward Krishna's head with all the force of his fury behind it, a blow powerful enough to crush a man's skull.

But Krishna was swift. He sidestepped the strike, the club whistling through the air where his head had been only moments before. Dantavakra growled in frustration and swung again, this time with more precision, aiming to catch Krishna off guard.

The clash of their weapons rang out like thunder, the force of their blows sending shockwaves through the ground. Dantavakra's eyes were wild, his breath coming in ragged gasps as he continued to attack, each strike more desperate than the last. But Krishna remained calm, his movements fluid, his strikes precise.

'You think you can defeat me, cousin?' Dantavakra spat, his voice thick with hatred. 'You are nothing! You are a disease, a blight on our family, and I will be the one to rid the world of you!'

Krishna's response was measured, his voice steady as he countered Dantavakra's onslaught. 'Your anger blinds you, Dantavakra. It has consumed you, just as it consumed Shishupal. You cannot win this fight, not with rage alone.'

'Lies!' Dantavakra roared, swinging his club with all his might. The force of the blow sent shockwaves through the ground, but Krishna was ready. With a swift motion, he blocked the strike with *Kaumodaki*, the impact reverberating through the air.

For a moment, the two cousins stood locked in place, their weapons clashing, their gazes locked in a silent battle of wills. Dantavakra's breath came in harsh gasps, his muscles straining with the effort of holding his ground, while Krishna remained calm, his strength unwavering.

And then, with a sudden burst of speed, Krishna broke the deadlock. He swung his club upward, striking Dantavakra's weapon with such force that it was torn from his hands and sent flying through the air, landing with a heavy thud several feet away.

Dantavakra staggered back, his chest heaving as he struggled to regain his balance. For the first time, a flicker of doubt crossed his face. 'You... you think this is over?' he snarled, though the words sounded hollow even to his own ears.

Without waiting for a response, he lunged at Krishna, his fists raised, his teeth bared in a snarl. But Krishna was faster. With a single, fluid motion, he brought *Kaumodaki* down upon Dantavakra's chest, the blow landing with a sickening crunch.

Dantavakra's eyes widened in shock as the force of the strike shattered his ribcage, the impact sending him reeling backward. He could feel his heart faltering, his lungs struggling to draw breath. Blood spurted from his mouth, staining the ground beneath him as he collapsed to his knees, his hands clutching at his chest.

'No…' he gasped, his voice weak, his strength failing him. 'This… this cannot be…'

'I offered you a chance to turn away from this path, cousin,' Krishna replied, his tone now one of solemnity. 'You chose to embrace the darkness.'

With a defiant roar, Dantavakra gathered what remained of his strength and stood up, gasping. His head spun as he bent down to retrieve his club, which lay in the dust. He rose up slowly, staggering and swaying. Breathing heavily, he steadied himself and declared loudly, 'I will not die like a coward!' he spat, raising his club once more. But his movements were sluggish now, each breath a labour as he struggled to remain on his feet.

With another swing of *Kaumodaki,* Krishna struck Dantavakra again, the sound of the impact echoing like a drumbeat of destiny. The blow landed with lethal precision upon his heart, crushing Dantavakra's spirit. The king's body crumpled to the ground, his club falling from his grasp, forgotten in the face of inevitable defeat.

Krishna knelt beside him, the weight of their shared blood lingering in the air, his gaze sorrowful as he looked down at his fallen cousin. 'Your anger led you here, Dantavakra. But it is not too late to find peace.'

Dantavakra's vision blurred and darkness crept in around him. His hands slipped from his chest, falling limply to his sides as his body slumped forward. The world around him grew distant, the sounds of the battlefield fading into a dull roar as his heartbeat slowed, then stopped.

For a moment, the battlefield was silent, the only sound being the soft rustle of the wind through the grass. And then, with a final, shuddering breath, Dantavakra's body collapsed to the ground, lifeless.

Krishna stood over him, his expression unreadable as he looked down at the fallen king. There was no triumph in his gaze, no sense of victory—only a quiet sadness, the weight of another life lost to the futility of vengeance.

He turned away, leaving Dantavakra's body where it lay, a stark reminder of the cost of unchecked rage. The sun dipped below the horizon, casting long shadows across the battlefield as Krishna made his way back to his chariot, the echoes of the battle fading into the distance.

As he walked away from the fallen Dantavakra, the weight of his cousin's choices lingered in his heart, a reminder of the fine line between vengeance and justice, and the true cost of unchecked ambition.

And so ended the reign of Dantavakra, the king of Karusha, brought low by his own anger and desire for vengeance. His story would be remembered for generations, a cautionary tale of the dangers of letting hatred rule the heart. Yet even in death, his name would live on, etched into the annals of history alongside those of his fallen friends Jarasandha and Shishupal, all victims of the same destructive path.

'Ah, mortals and gods who listen, hear of the brothers born from the mingling of asuric fire and divine grace, each of us shaped by forces far greater than ourselves. I, Ravana, King of Lanka, stand here on the battlefield, the weight of destiny heavy upon me. My brother Kumbhakarna, the indomitable force of nature, lies felled, and my heart is darkened not only by the doom we face but by the betrayal of our own blood–Vibhishana.

'We three were born of Vishrava, a sage of unparalleled wisdom, and Kaikesi, an asura queen of unyielding will. This lineage split our souls in two–one part divine, the other demonic. From the moment we entered this world, the seeds of greatness and ruin were sown in us. I, the eldest, embraced the might and ambition of our asura blood. I was destined to conquer, to stand above gods and men alike. My mastery over the Vedas and the boons I gained from Brahma and Shiva were but steps toward my ultimate goal: dominion over the three worlds. Lanka, which I seized from our half-brother Kubera, became a fortress of unmatched grandeur, its walls thick with the might of our asuric blood.

'Kumbhakarna, my loyal brother, stood beside me through it all. Though monstrous in form and cursed with endless sleep, his heart was pure in its devotion. He fought not for power, not for conquest, but for me, for the blood we shared. His immense strength, feared by all who heard his name, was never used in cruelty for its own sake. He lived and died in the service of his brother, blind to his own tragedy.

'And then there is Vibhishana. He, too, was shaped by our mixed lineage, but his heart leaned toward the dharma of our father's side. He saw the world differently, driven not by ambition

but by a desire for righteousness. Yet what is righteousness to us who walk in the path of power? When the winds of war blew and Rama, the prince of Ayodhya, stood before our gates, Vibhishana chose his side. He did not see Rama as a god, but as a man of virtue, a king bound by the moral laws Vibhishana held so dear. He could not see that in this world, it is power, not righteousness, that shapes fate. Vibhishana's vision of dharma could never stand beside the asuric fire that burns within Kumbhakarna and me.

'Yet now, I realise, we are not feared simply for the strength in our arms or the kingdoms we crushed. We became the terrible asuras of legend because we dared to defy the very order of existence. I sought to rise above gods and mortals alike, to bend fate to my will, and in doing so, I became a symbol of everything that terrifies the worlds—the unchecked ambition that burns through all bonds of family, of blood, of love.

'Kumbhakarna's heart was pure. Mine was filled with the fire of conquest. But it is Vibhishana, the righteous fool, who will live on—as the traitor who turned away from that fire, to serve a mortal king in the name of justice.'

—Ravana, Emperor of Lanka

THIRTEEN

Dark Union

The Sage and the Rakshasa Princess

In the twilight of a world born of myth and power, Brahma, the Creator, sat atop his luminous lotus throne, his vast consciousness spreading out in all directions, weaving the very fabric of existence. From his mind, he brought forth the *Prajapatis*, the progenitors of life. Among these celestial beings were luminaries like Daksha, Vasishtha, and the enigmatic Narada. Yet, the one who would play a pivotal role in the destiny of the Rakshasas was the great sage Pulastya. Pulastya, a being of immense wisdom, fathered two sons: Agastya, a towering figure among rishis, and Vishrava, whose destiny would intertwine with the dark forces of the world.

Vishrava, with his unmatched penance, lived in his hermitage, far removed from the machinations of the world. He was a sage who commanded the respect of gods and demons alike. He had taken a wife, Ilavida, and together they had a son, Kubera, the Lord of Wealth. Vishrava's life was steeped in righteousness, his days spent in meditation and deep spiritual practice, and Kubera, under his guidance, rose to great prominence in the celestial realms.

Far from the peaceful serenity of Vishrava's hermitage, in the shadowy depths of Patala, lay the kingdom of Rakshasas, a race of beings who thrived in chaos and bloodshed. Their king, Sumali, a figure of towering strength and cunning, brooded upon his decaying throne. His kingdom, once a bastion of Rakshasa might, was waning. The line of Rakshasas was weakening, their powers diminishing with every generation. There were no sons to carry on the dark legacy. Sumali's heart burned with the desire to restore his race to its former glory, to produce an heir who could stand against the gods themselves.

In the dimly lit court of Sumali, a council of Rakshasa ministers convened. 'The Rakshasa race is growing weak,' one minister declared, his voice thick with concern. 'We need progeny of great power, ones who will restore our kingdom and strike fear into the hearts of men and gods.'

Sumali's brows furrowed. 'But who can bring forth such a child?' he asked, his voice echoing through the shadowed hall.

'We need not look for Rakshasas alone,' the chief minister said. 'The sages, those of great *tejobala* (spiritual strength), hold the power of creation and destruction. If we were to seek one of their kind, perhaps the offspring born of such a union would possess the might to lead us to greatness.'

The court buzzed with agreement, and the discussion shifted to finding the perfect sage. Many names were put forth, but after days of deliberation, the name of Vishrava arose. A rishi of such immense spiritual potency, they reasoned, could father children capable of unimaginable power.

Sumali's daughter, Kaikesi, listened intently to the discussion. Her heart burned with ambition, and her dark beauty was matched only by her cunning. The ministers spoke of her marrying Vishrava, for he alone could father the Rakshasa king they needed. Kaikesi, resolute and determined, agreed.

'I shall go to him,' she said, her voice calm but filled with resolve. 'I will ensure that this union takes place. Our future depends on it.'

Thus, with her father's blessing, Kaikesi set out with her entourage toward Vishrava's hermitage. As they approached the sage's abode, surrounded by towering trees and the soft murmur of sacred chants, Kaikesi's resolve strengthened. This was her destiny, and she would see it fulfilled.

When the entourage arrived at the peaceful hermitage, Vishrava emerged from his meditation, his aura glowing with divine energy. His eyes fell upon Kaikesi and her retinue. He recognised her for what she was—Rakshasa blood flowed through her veins, and her beauty, though striking, could not mask the darkness within her.

Kaikesi, with all the grace of a queen, approached Vishrava. 'O great sage, I have come to seek your hand in marriage,' she said, her voice a blend of honeyed tones and hidden menace. 'I, Kaikesi, daughter of Sumali, offer myself to you.'

Vishrava's eyes narrowed. He could see through the veil of her beauty and her sweet words. He knew of the Rakshasas, their ways, their thirst for power. 'This union is ill-fated,' he said, his voice calm yet firm. 'The stars themselves are misaligned for such a marriage. Your blood and mine are not meant to mingle.'

Kaikesi was undeterred. 'But my lord,' she pleaded, 'together, we can create a lineage of unmatched power. The children born from our union will be invincible.'

'The time is not right,' Vishrava repeated. 'I cannot agree to this.'

Kaikesi was not one to give up so easily. She knew that a direct approach would not work with Vishrava. Over the next few days, she lingered at the hermitage, observing the sage from a distance, waiting for the perfect opportunity. One night, as Vishrava performed his evening rites, Kaikesi attempted to seduce him, using every art of persuasion known to her. She adorned herself in the finest silks, her dark eyes glittering in the firelight, her voice a soft murmur in the night air.

But Vishrava remained unmoved.

As days passed, Kaikesi's resolve only grew stronger. She devised a final plan—one that would force Vishrava's hand. One evening, as Vishrava sat deep in his meditations, preparing for a powerful yajna, Kaikesi approached him once more. This time, she waited until the ritual had begun, a time when the sage could not break his silence nor refuse any request. She stood before him, her voice soft yet filled with determination. 'Marry me, O great sage,' she implored, her eyes gleaming with victory. 'For I, Kaikesi, have waited long for this union.'

Bound by the sacred rites of the yajna, Vishrava could not refuse her. His heart burned with anger at being trapped in such a way, but he had no choice. 'Very well,' he said, his voice filled with fury. 'But know this—this union is cursed. The children born of this bond shall tread the path of *adharma* (unrighteousness). They shall be beings of immense power, but their hearts will be dark, filled with cruelty and deceit.'

Kaikesi's heart trembled at these words, but she pressed on. 'Please, my lord,' she begged, 'do not curse our offspring. I ask for forgiveness.'

Vishrava, seeing the sincerity in her plea, relented slightly. 'The curse shall remain,' he said, 'but the last child born to us will be an exception. He shall walk the path of righteousness, unlike his siblings.'

In time, Kaikesi bore four children—Dashagreeva, Kumbhakarna, Minakshi, and Vibhishana. As each child was born, the prophecy of Vishrava echoed through the halls of the Rakshasa kingdom. The first three were born with immense power and ambition, their hearts darkened by the curse of their father. Dashagreeva, in particular, was a child of remarkable strength and intelligence, but his soul was restless, his ambitions limitless.

Yet, when Vibhishana was born, a sense of calm descended upon the household. This child, unlike his siblings, was born with a heart inclined towards *dharma*, a being of righteousness in a family shrouded in darkness.

Vishrava watched his children grow from a distance, his heart heavy with the weight of the curse. He saw in Dashagreeva the seeds of destruction, the potential for greatness marred by an insatiable thirst for power. And in Vibhishana, he saw the light of dharma flickering in the shadow of his elder brother's ambitions.

As time passed, the tension between half-brothers Kubera and Dashagreeva became palpable in Vishrava's ashram. Kubera, the elder son of Vishrava and Ilavida, was the revered God of Wealth, governing his prosperous city, Alakapuri, with wisdom and fairness. Kubera embodied the ideals of dharma, austerity, and devotion to his duties as a custodian of wealth. He had inherited the brilliance of his father, Vishrava, and his demeanour exuded calm authority. Dashagreeva, however, felt only disdain for Kubera.

To Dashagreeva, Kubera's calm temperament and lack of ambition were signs of weakness. Where Kubera saw harmony in prosperity, Dashagreeva saw only missed opportunities. His heart brimmed with the desire for power—power to rule not just a city or a kingdom, but to dominate worlds, deities, and the heavens themselves. Every word Kubera spoke about *dharma* or restraint further fanned the flames of Dashagreeva's contempt.

Vibhishana often gravitated toward Kubera, soaking in his wisdom and observing his restrained approach to power. In contrast, Kumbhakarna—possessing immense physical strength—was closer to Dashagreeva, constantly nudged by his elder brother toward thoughts of conquest and war.

Sumali saw immense potential in his grandchildren, particularly in Dashagreeva, the eldest son. He bore all the signs of a future ruler—tenacious, sharp-minded, with the determination to shape the cosmos to his will. Kaikesi, nurturing her ambition to see her sons as conquerors, wanted to raise them in her father's court. After all, Sumali was known for his wisdom in matters of warfare and power, traits she wanted her sons to inherit. But her husband Vishrava, having already foreseen their destinies, was against it.

Vishrava, though an ascetic, knew the allure of power and its consequences. He saw early signs in Dashagreeva's nature as the boy had already begun to display a thirst for control that troubled him deeply. Kaikesi, ever determined to restore the Rakshasa dynasty to its former glory, became uneasy as she watched her sons grow up under Vishrava's tutelage. While she respected the sage's authority and knowledge, her ultimate loyalty was to the Rakshasa bloodline. She recognised in Dashagreeva the strength, ambition, and cunning that could lead the Rakshasas to reclaim their lost dominance. However, Vishrava understood that leaving them under Sumali's influence would lead them down a dangerous path.

'No, Kaikesi,' Vishrava said one day as they discussed their children's futures. 'Our children stay with me.'

Kaikesi frowned, her dark eyes gleaming with resistance. 'But the children belong with my people. They need to learn the ways of the Rakshasas, how to survive and thrive in a world that fears them.' Her voice was smooth but firm.

Vishrava stood unyielding. 'Dashagreeva, Kumbhakarna, and Minakshi will follow their destinies as you wish, but Vibhishana is different. His heart is pure, and I will not let him be corrupted by Sumali's ambitions.' Vishrava's voice bore the weight of the prophecy he had laid upon his offspring.

Kaikesi knew better than to argue further. Vishrava was not a man who could be easily swayed, and she had already succeeded in bending his will when she had first manipulated him into marriage. She could not push her luck again. Yet her heart sank, knowing that by keeping the children with their father, she would not be able to groom them as she desired. However, Sumali had a solution. Vishrava went away for long periods of austerities, often for months at a time. Kaikesi convinced him to allow her to go with the children to her father's home in Patala during those times and he reluctantly agreed. Sumali used these periods to inculcate Rakshasa values into the children.

Under the watchful eyes of Sumali, Dashagreeva's latent power began to take form. In Patala, the young boy was exposed to the grand vision of Rakshasa power and ambition, where might was honoured above all else. Under Sumali's influence, Dashagreeva began to understand the depths of his lineage's legacy and felt a deeper connection to his ancestral roots. Sumali began teaching him the ancient techniques of the Rakshasas, their mastery of deception, war, and manipulation. The young boy was a quick learner and absorbed it all eagerly, but more than anything, Dashagreeva grew obsessed with the stories of the Devas and the power they held over the worlds. In particular, the wealth and prosperity of the heavens stirred a deep resentment within him.

Vibhishana felt torn between his affection for his brothers and his understanding of dharma. While he recognised the ambition that fuelled Dashagreeva and Kumbhakarna, he believed he could still influence them to choose the righteous path. Vibhishana had learned much about the importance of *tapasya* from Vishrava. He knew that a disciplined mind, free from greed and hatred, was capable of achieving unimaginable strength.

'Power through devotion, not through destruction,' Vibhishana would often say to his brothers, whenever they met. 'Austerity sharpens the spirit; it brings us closer to the divine, to wisdom.'

His brothers, however, were not easily swayed. Though Kumbhakarna respected Vibhishana's wisdom, he was more drawn to Dashagreeva's vision of conquest. Dashagreeva was convinced that strength was all that mattered, and he began to seek out ways to harness his power through any means necessary.

While Dashagreeva's ambitions grew, Kumbhakarna developed in a completely different way. From a young age, his size and strength were unmatched. He could crush boulders with his bare hands and uproot trees as easily as plucking flowers. But with his immense power came an equally immense hunger. Kumbhakarna's appetite was insatiable, and he was known to devour entire herds of animals in a single meal. Despite his strength, there was something gentle about Kumbhakarna, a childlike innocence that often made him seem out of place in the ruthless world of the Rakshasas.

Minakshi, on the other hand, displayed a wild and ferocious spirit from her earliest days. She was quick to anger and quicker to violence, often lashing out at those who displeased her. Yet she was also cunning, using her beauty to manipulate those around her. Even as a child, Minakshi showed signs of the viciousness that would later define her. She revelled in causing pain, whether it was tormenting animals or playing cruel tricks on other Rakshasas.

While Kumbhakarna found solace in food and rest, Minakshi sought power in cruelty. She would often watch as Dashagreeva trained with Sumali, yearning to join in but knowing that her brothers did not yet take her seriously. She vowed that one day they would respect her, not just as their sister but as a force to be reckoned with.

Sumali watched Dashagreeva grow, subtly steering him away from his father's influence and toward the ways of the Rakshasas. While Vishrava had taught Dashagreeva the sacred texts and imbued in him a deep understanding of the Vedas, Sumali stoked the fires of ambition in his grandson's heart. He instilled in Dashagreeva the belief that power was to be seized through might.

In the quiet halls of Sumali's court, Dashagreeva often heard of his half-brother, Kubera, the god of wealth, who ruled from Lanka, a city of unmatched splendour and prosperity. The more he heard, the more a seed of resentment grew in Dashagreeva's mind. Why should Kubera, the son of the same father, live a life of abundance while he and his siblings were exiled to the shadowy realms of Patala?

'Grandfather,' young Dashagreeva asked Sumali one evening, his voice low but intense, 'why should Kubera hold the throne of Lanka? I think that the wealth of Lanka should belong to those who have the strength to defend it.'

Sumali, who had a penchant for wine, was quite drunk by then, and his eyes were heavy with sleep. Somehow, he managed to mumble, 'Lanka once belonged to us.' His voice was laced with bitterness. 'That *Yaksha* has no place in our Lanka. 'You, Dashagreeva, will get our homeland back.'

'Our homeland? What are you saying grandfather?' Dashagreeva wanted to know. But the old Rakshasa was already asleep.

FOURTEEN

Dashagreeva's Hubris

A Crushing Defeat

Deep within the labyrinthine caverns of Rasatala, where shadows danced like dark nymphs and torches cast a flickering golden glow, seventeen-year-old Dashagreeva stood tall, his head held high, as he listened to Sumali's words of caution. The dimly lit caverns of Rasatala, the underworld realm, seemed to amplify the gravity of his grandfather's tone.

'Dashagreeva, you are young and impulsive,' Sumali warned, his voice laced with concern. 'Kartavirya Arjuna is no ordinary foe. His conquests are legendary, and his strength unmatched.'

Dashagreeva's jaw clenched, his dark hair whipping around his face like a wild aura. 'I will not be swayed, grandfather. I will prove myself worthy of our Rakshasa legacy. The whispers of Kartavirya's invincibility only fuel my determination.'

Sumali's voice took on a tone of worn leather, soft but unyielding. 'Your arrogance will be your downfall, Dashagreeva. You have much to learn, and the price of pride is steep.'

But Dashagreeva's heart remained unmoved, his

resolve forged in the fires of ambition. As he navigated the serpentine tunnels of Rasatala, Dashagreeva encountered clusters of Rakshasa warriors. Their whispers followed him like a swarm of biting insects.

'...full of hot air, that one...'

'...thinks himself a king already...'

'...will crash and burn, mark my words.'

Dashagreeva's ears burned with resentment, but his stride remained purposeful. He sought out Maricha, the revered Rakshasa sorcerer, whose eyes shone with ancient wisdom. Maricha's lair radiated a serene aura, filled with the scent of sandalwood and sacred herbs.

'O Maricha,' Dashagreeva said, his voice laced with reverence. 'I seek your counsel. I wish to challenge Kartavirya Arjuna and prove my worth.'

Maricha's gaze pierced the shadows, his voice low and measured. 'Dashagreeva, the fire that burns within you is both your strength and weakness. Ambition can fuel greatness, but untempered, it consumes the soul.'

'Yet, Guru, is it not our duty to assert our power?' Dashagreeva asked, his brow furrowed.

Maricha's eyes seemed to hold the weight of centuries. 'Power, yes. But at what cost? The true measure of strength lies not in conquest, but in self-mastery. Conquer your own self, Dashagreeva, before seeking to vanquish others.'

Dashagreeva's face twisted in frustration. 'But how can I prove myself, Guru?'

Maricha's expression turned compassionate. 'Prove yourself to yourself, Dashagreeva. The world will recognise your worth when you have earned it within. Heed my words, young one, the greatest battles are fought within.'

Dashagreeva's face hardened, his mind already made up. 'I will not be deterred, Guru. I will show Kartavirya Arjuna the true meaning of Rakshasa power.'

Maricha's gaze pierced the veil of Dashagreeva's arrogance. 'You aren't ready yet, Dashagreeva. You need to learn to control your own weaknesses. Kartavirya Arjuna will exploit your unpreparedness, and you will fall.'

Dashagreeva's anger flared, his face reddening. 'You doubt me, Guru?'

Maricha's voice remained calm, his words laced with a deeper truth. 'I doubt your readiness, Dashagreeva. You have not yet faced the mirror of your own soul. When you do, you will see the true enemy.'

Dashagreeva's laughter echoed through the cavern, sending shivers down Maricha's spine.

'You should know, Maricha,' Dashagreeva said, his voice dripping with malice, daring now to call the wise elder by his name. 'My father Vishrava's Rishi wisdom courses through my veins.'

Maricha's expression became grave as his gaze locked onto Dashagreeva. 'You tap into powers beyond your understanding, Dashagreeva. Your mixed heritage—Rakshasa and Rishi—holds unpredictable powers.'

Dashagreeva's smile twisted. 'I will unlock its secrets, and none will stand in my way.'

As Dashagreeva turned to go, the sorcerer's voice followed him, filled with a mix of sorrow and foreboding.

'May your conscience guide you, Dashagreeva,' Maricha whispered to himself. 'For the path you have chosen leads to either greatness or destruction. The threads of fate are complex, but one thing is certain: your destiny is intertwined with the fate of Lanka, and the future of our realm.'

Dashagreeva stormed through the winding tunnels of Rasatala, his anger and frustration simmering like a cauldron left unattended. Maricha's words echoed in his mind, fuelling his resentment.

'How dare he doubt me?' Dashagreeva seethed, his fists clenched. 'I will show him, show them all, my true power.'

As he walked, the shadows seemed to deepen, reflecting the darkness growing within him. His footsteps quickened; his breathing heavy with agitation.

Suddenly, a figure emerged from the shadows: Vibhishana, his younger brother. Vibhishana's calm demeanour only infuriated Dashagreeva further.

'Vibhishana, what do you want?' Dashagreeva snapped, his voice biting.

Vibhishana's eyes widened, concern etched on his face. 'Brother, I sensed your turmoil. What troubles you?'

Dashagreeva's laughter was cold, mirthless. 'Maricha's doubts, that's all. He thinks I'm weak, foolish.'

Vibhishana's expression turned gentle. 'Maricha seeks to guide you, brother. Heed his words.'

Dashagreeva's anger boiled over, his face twisted in rage. 'You too? You doubt me?'

Without warning, Dashagreeva turned and struck the nearest torch, sending flames dancing across the cavern wall. The fiery blaze seemed to mirror the turmoil within him.

'I will show them all,' Dashagreeva vowed, his voice

dripping with malice. 'I will challenge Kartavirya Arjuna, and no one will stop me.'

Vibhishana's eyes filled with sorrow, his voice barely above a whisper. 'Brother, you walk the path of destruction.'

Dashagreeva's response was a cold, calculated smile. 'Watch me, Vibhishana. Watch me burn the world.'

As Dashagreeva emerged from the caverns, the scorching sun beat down upon his skin, but he felt no discomfort. His focus remained fixed on the challenge ahead.

Dashagreeva traversed the arid landscape, his footsteps steady and purposeful. The wind whipped his dark hair into a frenzy, but his eyes remained unwavering. He crossed rivers, climbed mountains, and braved treacherous forests, undaunted by the perils that lay before him. After many days of travel, Dashagreeva arrived at the outskirts of Mahishmati, Kartavirya Arjuna's kingdom. The city's walls rose majestically, its gates guarded by formidable warriors.

With deliberate strides, he approached the city gates, his presence commanding attention.

A burly gatekeeper blocked Dashagreeva's path, hand on the hilt of his sword. 'Who dares to disturb the peace of Mahishmati?'

Dashagreeva's eyes flashed with defiance. 'I am Dashagreeva, son of Vishrava. I have come to challenge Kartavirya Arjuna.'

The guardian's expression turned sceptical. 'You are either brave or foolhardy.'

Dashagreeva's laughter echoed through the gates. 'I am both.'

The guardian's expression turned grave. 'I will inform King Kartavirya Arjuna of your challenge. But be warned Dashagreeva, our king is not one to be underestimated.'

Dashagreeva's smile remained, his confidence unwavering. 'I do not underestimate him. But I will conquer him.'

The guardian disappeared into the city, leaving Dashagreeva standing before the gates. The sun beat down upon his skin as time passed, and Dashagreeva's anticipation grew. He sensed the weight of his destiny unfolding.

The city gates swung open, and Kartavirya Arjuna stepped forth. He radiated authority, his eyes gleaming with a warrior's intensity.

'Dashagreeva, son of Vishrava,' Kartavirya Arjuna said, his voice deep and commanding. 'I have heard your boasts. Come, let us see if your strength matches your words.'

Dashagreeva bowed, his gesture laced with mockery. 'I will show you my strength, Kartavirya Arjuna. And when I emerge victorious, all will know my name.'

The two warriors faced each other, their eyes locked in a fierce stare. The air seemed to vibrate with tension, the outcome hanging precariously in the balance.

Kartavirya Arjuna drew his sword, its blade shimmering in the sunlight. Dashagreeva smiled, his hands weaving intricate patterns in the air.

The duel commenced, each warrior unleashing their unique abilities. The clash of steel and sorcery echoed through the city, signalling the start of a legendary confrontation.

Dashagreeva unleashed a barrage of dark energy, but Kartavirya Arjuna stood unfazed. The legendary warrior's aura repelled the sorcery, rendering it ineffective.

'You rely too heavily on tricks, Dashagreeva,' Kartavirya Arjuna said, his sword flashing in the sunlight. 'True strength lies in the arm and the heart.'

Dashagreeva's eyes narrowed, his confidence undeterred. He drew his own sword, its blade forged from the darkest metals.

The two warriors engaged, their swords clashing in a flurry of strikes. Dashagreeva's skills were formidable, but Kartavirya Arjuna's prowess was unmatched. The duel raged on, neither opponent yielding. As the battle wore on, Dashagreeva's frustration grew. Kartavirya Arjuna sensed his opponent's doubt and pressed his advantage. Immediately, Dashagreeva charged forward, his sword flashing in the sunlight. 'You're no match for me, Kartavirya Arjuna! I'll show you the true meaning of power!'

Kartavirya Arjuna smiled, his eyes glinting with amusement. 'Your arrogance is misplaced, Dashagreeva. Your ambition exceeds your strength. Remember this defeat.'

With a swift swing Kartavirya Arjuna sent Dashagreeva crashing to the ground. The young warrior scrambled to rise but Kartavirya Arjuna's blows rained down relentlessly. Dashagreeva crumbled beneath the onslaught. Kartavirya Arjuna's attacks came faster, each blow landing with unyielding force.

Dashagreeva's sword flew from his grasp, shattered by Kartavirya Arjuna's relentless assault. The young warrior gasped, his vision blurring.

Kartavirya Arjuna stood over him, his chest heaving with exertion. 'You dared challenge me, Dashagreeva. You will not forget this lesson soon.'

As Dashagreeva struggled to stand, Kartavirya Arjuna kicked him hard, sending him tumbling once more. Then, seizing him by the scruff, Kartavirya Arjuna lifted him high, and hurled him into the air.

'Fly, little Rakshasa!' Kartavirya Arjuna roared, laughter echoing through the land.

Dashagreeva flew across the face of the earth, finally crashing onto the dusty grounds of Mahishmati, his clothes tattered, his body bruised. The people of Mahishmati gathered, their faces filled with mirth, their jeers stinging Dashagreeva's pride. Kartavirya Arjuna ordered his soldiers to lock Dashagreeva up in a cage and keep it on public display in one corner of the marketplace.

Pulastya, Dashagreeva's wise grandfather, was meditating on the banks of Narmada in his Ashram, close to the city of Mahishmati. As soon as he came to know of the capture and confinement of Dashagreeva, he rushed to meet Kartavirya Arjuna, who greatly respected Brahma's son. At Pulastya's behest Kartavirya Arjuna released the young boy, but with a stern warning.

Pulastya addressed his grandson, shaking his head. 'Your arrogance has earned you this, Dashagreeva. Learn from your mistakes.'

As Dashagreeva crawled out of the cage, his face twisted in a scowl, the seeds of resentment took root within him. 'I will not forget this humiliation,' Dashagreeva vowed, his heart burning with hatred.

Pulastya watched his angst-ridden grandson storm away, never to return.

Once back at Rasatala, a fuming Dashagreeva nursed his wounded pride. His ego bruised, he struggled to come to terms with his defeat. Soon, he started engaging in a series of fights with his own Rakshasa kin, seeking to prove his strength. However, his victories were hollow, and his brethren began to mock him.

'You seek glory among your own?' they taunted. 'Go test your mettle elsewhere, Dashagreeva.'

Undeterred, young Dashagreeva turned his attention to the forests and mountains. He hunted and battled fearsome beasts, seeking to assert his dominance. His anger and resentment toward Kartavirya Arjuna and his own Rakshasa brethren simmered, fuelling his determination to prove them wrong. He began doubting if he had actually inherited his father's wisdom and strength or merely his pride. Was he the mighty warrior he claimed to be, or just a pretender?

'Who am I, truly?'

Dashagreeva gradually retreated into a dark silence, refusing food and words. His chamber became a prison, where shadows danced with his despair. Kaikesi, worried for her son, sought her father Sumali's guidance.

'Father, please help Dashagreeva,' Kaikesi implored.

'He's lost to his own darkness.'

Sumali, wise and compassionate, visited Dashagreeva's chambers. He found the young Rakshasa shrouded in darkness. Sumali approached Dashagreeva slowly, his voice gentle. 'My child, your lineage is noble, your potential vast. Why let defeat define you?'

Sumali spoke of their ancestors, mighty Rakshasas who commanded respect. 'You carry their blood, Dashagreeva. Remember your heritage.'

'I think of you as a great leader,' Sumali said, his eyes locked on Dashagreeva's. 'One who would unite our kind and bring glory to our name.'

Dashagreeva's silence began to crack. Sumali's words stirred a spark within him.

'In what way, grandfather?' Dashagreeva whispered, his voice barely audible.

Sumali smiled, his eyes glinting. 'The path to greatness lies not in brute strength, but in attaining true power. Forge powerful alliances. Seek great powers from those who can bestow boons, and you shall achieve your desires.'

Dashagreeva's interest grew. He sensed a new path unfolding. 'Tell me more, grandfather,' Dashagreeva urged, his voice gaining strength. Sumali's counsel had awakened Dashagreeva from his darkness.

'Seek out and make friends, Dashagreeva. Powerful friends.' Sumali said quietly, 'every battle is not won by brute force alone.'

Dashagreeva began to go out once again with the other Rakshasas. Very soon, he forgot Sumali's sage advice and his conquests over kings started once again. In time, he set his sights on the Vanaras, seeking to prove his superiority over Vali, the Vanara king. Dashagreeva's search for the Vanara king led him to the ocean's shore, where Vali was deeply engrossed in worship.

Unnoticed, Dashagreeva crept up behind Vali, intent on launching a surprise attack. However, Vali's keen senses alerted him to the lurking danger. With lightning speed, Vali grasped Dashagreeva and exclaimed, 'Caught you!' The monkey-king tucked the Rakshasa under his arm and soared into the sky.

Below, Dashagreeva's Rakshasa forces witnessed his predicament and gave chase. Vali's incredible agility and strength, however, was no match for them and they were left far behind. As Vali flew around the world, Dashagreeva struggled to free himself. Eventually, Vali landed, releasing Dashagreeva from his grasp.

'Strength is not solely in the arm, Dashagreeva. It lies in the heart and the mind.'

Vali's words struck a chord. Dashagreeva saw the futility of his pride and the value of humility. Breathless and humbled, Dashagreeva addressed Vali with newfound respect. 'I want to be your friend, great monkey!' he said.

Vali's hearty laughter echoed through the landscape. 'Very well, Dashagreeva. Let us forge an alliance. Together, our strength will be unmatched.'

Thus, the unlikely duo formed a bond, bridging their differences. Vali, aware of Dashagreeva's volatile nature, cautioned him, 'Friendship demands trust and loyalty. Remember, true strength lies not in conquest, but in harmony.'

Dashagreeva nodded, his mind racing with the possibilities. For the first time, he saw the value in alliances over domination. His grandfather Sumali had advised him well. As their friendship grew, Vali shared his wisdom with Dashagreeva, teaching him the importance of balance and cooperation.

At Sumali's urging, his grandsons decided to undertake a great *tapasya,* a gruelling ascetic practice aimed at acquiring boons from the gods on Mount Gokarna.

Vibhishana, guided by Vishrava, sought to use this as an opportunity to align his brothers with *dharma.* However, it hadn't occurred to him that one could choose to perform these tough ascetic practices to attain results far different from his own. Dashagreeva and Kumbhakarna had been given thorough instructions by Sumali before embarking upon their *tapasya.* They harboured very different motives from their guileless brother.

After a long period of austerity, Lord Brahma appeared before the brothers, pleased with their devotion. Brahma's voice echoed through the mountains, 'I am pleased with your penance. Ask what you desire, and it shall be granted.'

Vibhishana stepped forward, his voice steady and humble. 'Grant me, O Lord, unwavering devotion to righteousness and *dharma,*' he asked. 'May I never stray from the path of virtue, and may I always serve the greater good.'

Brahma smiled and granted Vibhishana's wish by uttering *'Tathastu'.* Though noble, it was not the kind of boon that would bring immediate power, and Dashagreeva looked upon his younger brother with scorn.

Next, it was Dashagreeva's turn. He had thought long and hard about what he would ask of Brahma. His words resonated with determination and arrogance as he made his demands.

'I, Dashagreeva, son of Vishrava and Kaikesi, seek supreme power!' he declared, his eyes glowing with fervour. 'Grant me immortality, O Lord of Creation, that no being, god, man, or beast may ever slay me!'

Brahma, knowing the consequences of such a boon, shook his head. 'Immortality I cannot grant. But ask of me anything else within the bounds of fate, and it shall be yours.'

Dashagreeva's mind raced, calculating. 'Then grant me this—let no god, no asura, no Rakshasa, no beast be able to kill me. Let me not die by the hands of those creatures created by you. Let my death not occur by any weapon forged by man or Deva, and let me not be slain either by day or night. Let me not perish on land or in the heavens.'

Brahma, impressed by the depth of Dashagreeva's request, granted the boon saying, *'Tathastu'*.

Then came Kumbhakarna's turn. The mighty Rakshasa, though strong, was not as calculating as Dashagreeva. His request, influenced by his gluttony, was initially to rule the heavens, but before he could fully articulate his wish, Saraswati, the goddess of wisdom and speech, intervened at Brahma's behest.

Saraswati whispered confusion into Kumbhakarna's mind, and instead of asking for dominion over the gods, Kumbhakarna mistakenly asked for eternal sleep. Brahma, respecting the rules of the boon, granted this request leaving Kumbhakarna to slumber for long periods, waking only briefly to satisfy his hunger before returning to sleep.

Dashagreeva was furious at the outcome, but he knew his own boon had secured his future. With the powers bestowed upon him, he would now have the strength to challenge the gods themselves.

FIFTEEN

Lanka Regained

The Many Shades of Hubris

Dashagreeva returned to Rasatala, fortified with Brahma's boons. His brethren Rakshasas regarded him with a mix of awe and fear. The boons had transformed Dashagreeva, imbuing him with unparalleled strength, cunning, and charisma. His eyes gleamed with an otherworldly intensity, striking awe in the hearts of his kin.

Sumali and Malyavan, Dashagreeva's granduncles, watched with keen interest, their faces etched with a mix of pride and trepidation. There was a fire in Dashagreeva, a thirst that could only be quenched by conquest. This was the moment he had been waiting for—the time to take back what was rightfully theirs.

'Dashagreeva, son of Vishrava,' Sumali began, his voice low and measured, 'your transformation is remarkable. Brahma's boons have indeed favoured you.'

'It has been a long and arduous journey, grandfather,' Dashagreeva spoke quietly, 'and I still have a long way to go.'

'Sit down, son,' Sumali continued, his voice deep and tinged with nostalgia. 'There is something you need to know—a truth that has been buried in the annals of time, a tale of loss and betrayal that only our blood remembers.'

Dashagreeva's eyes narrowed, he turned and faced the old king. Slowly, he lowered himself to the floor, folding his legs beneath him. His massive frame cast long shadows on the stone walls.

Sumali leaned back, his gaze fixed on the glowing embers of the fire before him. 'Lanka,' he began, his voice soft but deliberate. 'The island that your half-brother Kubera now rules was not always a city of Yakshas. Long before he claimed it, it was ours—the jewel of the Rakshasas. A city that was given to us by Brahma himself.'

Dashagreeva frowned. He had always known Lanka as Kubera's domain, but the thought that it once belonged to his own kin was both surprising and enraging.

Sumali continued, his voice a wistful echo of the past. 'The city of Lanka was not built by any mortal hands. It was crafted by the divine architect, Vishwakarma, at the request of none other than Shiva himself.'

Dashagreeva turned toward his grandfather with interest. 'Shiva? The Destroyer asked for this city to be built?'

'Indeed,' Sumali nodded. 'When the goddess Parvati, his beloved consort, asked for a grand home, Shiva commanded Vishwakarma to build Lanka. Vishwakarma, with his unparalleled skill, created this island city—a jewel of unmatched beauty and strength, fortified by oceans on all sides. Its spires, its fortifications, the wealth that lined its streets—all were the result of his heavenly craftsmanship. But it was not the Yakshas who were its first rulers. No, Lanka was forged for us, the Rakshasas, in a time when we held sway over vast territories. Lanka is our ancestral home. My brothers, Mali and Malyavan, and I, we were its rightful lords.'

Dashagreeva frowned, his hands clenched into fists. He felt immense anger swirling within him. 'Then how did Kubera, a mere Yaksha, come to sit upon its throne?'

'Ah, Dashagreeva, my dear grandson,' Sumali sighed deeply, as though the memory of the loss still pained him. 'When the palace was completed, Vishrava, your father, was asked to conduct the consecration ceremony. The *grihapravesh* was a grand affair, and after the rituals, Vishrava, in his wisdom, asked for Lanka as *dakshina*—And then, without a thought, he gifted it to his son Kubera, that cunning Yaksha king.'

Dashagreeva could feel the injustice gnawing at his insides. His own father had given Lanka to Kubera! Why didn't he rule it himself? Dashagreeva felt it was his legacy that had been stolen. 'And why did you all do nothing?' Dashagreeva growled. 'Why did you allow yourselves to be driven out like cowards?'

Sumali's face darkened, his eyes gleaming with an old bitterness. 'We fought hard. Your granduncle Mali, brave and fearless, challenged the gods themselves. His valour was unmatched, but alas, he fell to Vishnu's cunning. The Devas feared our growing influence and knew that if we retained control of the island, we would become unstoppable. Mali's defeat was their victory. After Mali's fall, we Rakshasas escaped from Lanka, seeking refuge in Rasatala.'

'Once we were forced to retreat, Kubera, the son

of Vishrava, your half-brother, came and sat on the golden throne of Lanka', Sumali spat the words out as though they were venom. 'The Yaksha has no right to that throne, for he is nothing more than a puppet of the gods. His wealth, his prosperity—it all stems from their favour.'

'Kubera's rule has brought darkness to Lanka. He has snuffed out the flames of our greatness, reduced our people to servitude. But I see in you, Dashagreeva, a spark of our ancient glory. Brahma's boons have made you powerful, and the fire of ambition burns inside you. Reclaim Lanka, Dashagreeva. Restore our honour, and bring back the days of Rakshasa supremacy.'

'We have waited, bided our time, hidden in the shadows until the moment was right to strike. And that moment has come, my grandson. You are the one who will reclaim Lanka and restore the glory of the Rakshasas.' Sumali's eyes gleamed with tears, his voice cracking with emotion, 'Lanka, our beloved home, calls to us. Will you answer, Dashagreeva?'

Dashagreeva's eyes blazed with a furious light. His destiny was clear now. He would reclaim Lanka, and in doing so, he would bring the Rakshasas back to their rightful place as the rulers of the world.

'But how, grandfather?' Dashagreeva asked, leaning forward. 'Kubera is protected by the gods. His wealth and his forces are vast. How can I defeat him?'

Sumali's lips curled into a smile. 'You have the blessings of Brahma, the creator himself. You are now invincible to gods, demons, and mortals alike. With your strength, no force can stand against you. The time has come for us to reclaim what is ours, but you must strike with both cunning and force.'

Dashagreeva rose to his feet, his expression grim. 'Then I will go to Lanka,' he declared. 'And I will take back what is mine.'

In the depths of Rasatala, Dashagreeva stood before the weakened Rakshasa forces, led by Prahastha. His voice echoed through the grand hall, stirring the embers of their forgotten glory.

'Brothers, we Rakshasas once ruled Lanka with might and wisdom. But we have forgotten our heritage, our strength dwindling like the ebbing tide. I call upon you, join me, and together we shall reclaim our birthright!'

The Rakshasas looked up, their eyes burning with a spark of hope. Dashagreeva's words ignited a fire within them, and they rallied behind their youthful leader.

Assembling a formidable naval force, Dashagreeva and his brother Kumbhakarna with him, set sail for Lanka. His fleet, a majestic armada of prows decorated with the fearsome faces of Rakshasa demons, cut through the waves like a sharp scimitar.

Meanwhile, Kubera, sensing the impending threat from his half-brother, sought counsel from their wise father. He travelled to Vishrava's ashram, nestled in the hilly forests, near the sacred river Narmada in his flying chariot, the *Pushpaka Vimana.* The wise sage received Kubera, his eyes filled with concern.

'Kubera, my son,' Vishrava said, 'Dashagreeva's resolve is unshakeable. His destiny is tied to Lanka's fate. Yield to him, and avoid bloodshed.'

Kubera knew to heed his father's words of wisdom. He returned to Lanka, prepared to abdicate, but only after trying to talk sense into his hot-headed half-brother.

As Dashagreeva's fleets neared the island, Lanka's golden towers gleamed in the distance, a stark contrast to the stormy skies. The air was thick with anticipation. Dashagreeva's heart raced with excitement as they approached, the thought of taking back what was his, filling him with a sense of destiny.

At the gates of Lanka, Kubera stood tall, flanked by his loyal Yaksha guards. Though he had heard rumours of his half-brother's growing power, he had never anticipated this—a menacing army of Rakshasas poured onto the beaches led by none other than Dashagreeva himself.

Astride his majestic chariot, Dashagreeva rode forth, his standard bearer hoisting the Rakshasa flag. The symbol of their ancestral glory fluttered in the wind, striking fear into the hearts of Kubera's Yakshas.

Kubera stepped forward, his voice calm but firm. 'Brother, what is the meaning of this? Why do you come here with an army? Lanka was given rightfully to me by our father.'

Dashagreeva smirked. 'Lanka is not yours, brother Kubera. It never was. The gods gave it to our father, but the land belonged to the Rakshasas. Our grandfather

Sumali was its true ruler, and now, by right of blood, I will take it back.'

Kubera's face darkened. He had always sensed the envy and bitterness in Dashagreeva's heart, but he had never imagined it would come to this. 'You would make war on your own brother? You would destroy the peace that our father, Vishrava, has worked so hard to build?'

'There can be no peace,' Dashagreeva hissed, his voice dripping with contempt, 'when you sit on a throne that was stolen from us. You have had your time, Kubera. Now, I will rule.'

'Very well, brother. Lanka is yours.'

Quietly, Kubera mounted his *Pushpaka Vimana* and left Lanka without a backward glance, honouring their father's advice, and leaving behind all his treasures. As Dashagreeva watched him go, he was initially confused at this turn of events. He took it to mean that Kubera was scared of him and ran away. The Yakshas departed for the Himalayas, and Dashagreeva claimed Lanka, restoring his family's honour.

Dashagreeva, seated upon the golden throne of Lanka, smiled with satisfaction as he looked out over his new kingdom. But even as he exulted in his victory, there was a subtle change in the atmosphere. Although Kubera had been driven out and the Rakshasas had regained their lost city, something about Lanka had shifted. The once vibrant city now seemed darker, its golden glow tinged with a sense of foreboding. The balance of power had been disturbed, and the consequences of that disturbance would ripple far beyond the borders of the island.

The mighty king convened with his council of elder Rakshasas. His piercing gaze, like the keen edge of a sword, swept across the assembly, beckoning their undivided attention.

'My lords, Lanka's complacency under Kubera's rule is bound to make us frail. The city's vulnerability to attacks was the reason we could overrun Lanka so easily. Now, this weakness threatens our very existence. We must immediately fortify our defences.'

Sumali, his venerable grandfather, nodded in agreement. 'The sea surrounds us, exposing our shores to naval invaders. We need robust coastal fortifications to safeguard our realm.'

Prahasta, a battle-hardened Rakshasa, spoke next. 'And, my lord, our open skies leave us vulnerable to aerial assaults. We must devise innovative defences to counter such threats.'

Dashagreeva's resolute face reflected his determination. 'We'll construct walls of unyielding stone, encircling Lanka like a shield. Watchtowers will rise along our coast, scanning the horizon for enemies. Submerged barriers will thwart hostile fleets.'

Sumali added, 'We need to establish a network of spies and scouts to gather intelligence on our enemies. Knowledge of their plans will grant us the foresight to prepare and counter their every move.'

The council's deliberations forged a master plan to make Lanka impregnable. Dashagreeva entrusted the task of redesigning Lanka's periphery to the most skilled

Rakshasa architects and engineers. Under the new king's supervision, the fortification project began. The earth was reshaped, and the city began to transform.

Dashagreeva stood at the threshold of a new era. His grandfather Sumali's wisdom and guidance had shaped him, but the weight of sovereignty now rested squarely on his shoulders.

However, whispers began to circulate about Dashagreeva's unpredictable temper. His rages shook the palace foundations, leaving even the bravest warriors trembling.

Dashagreeva marched on relentlessly, conquering kingdom after kingdom. He soon reached Ayodhya, ruled by King Anaranya, a descendant of the illustrious Ikshvaku. As Dashagreeva's armies approached, Anaranya prepared for battle, determined to defend his kingdom.

The two forces clashed, with Dashagreeva unleashing his formidable powers. Anaranya's army was no match for the Rakshasa king's sorcery, and they were swiftly defeated. Anaranya, however, refused to yield. He launched a fierce counter-attack, firing hundreds of arrows at Dashagreeva, but the latter's impenetrable armour repelled them all.

Undeterred, Anaranya continued to fight, but Dashagreeva's superior strength eventually prevailed. With a crushing blow, Dashagreeva struck Anaranya on the head, knocking him to the ground.

As Anaranya lay dying, he summoned his last ounce of strength to curse Dashagreeva. 'An avenger will arise from this very land of Ayodhya!' he declared, foretelling the arrival of a hero who would ultimately bring Dashagreeva's reign to an end. This avenger would be Rama, the son of Dasharatha. Dasharatha's lineage traced back to Anaranya through his son Khatvanga, followed by Dileepa, Raghu, and Aja.

One day, Dashagreeva was wandering through the forests and stumbled upon a serene scene. A beautiful woman, clad in a deer-skin, her hair twisted in *jatas,* sat in profound contemplation beside a fire-altar. Her focus was unwavering, her spirit radiant.

Dashagreeva, intrigued by her beauty and determination, approached her. 'Lovely lady,' he said, his voice laced with charm, 'you should adorn yourself with silks and jewels, not this austere garb. Be my wife, and share in my kingdom's splendour.'

The woman, Vedavati, lifted her gaze, her eyes burning with an inner fire. 'I am devoted to Lord Vishnu,' she declared, her voice firm. 'I will marry no other.'

Dashagreeva, unaccustomed to rejection, was taken aback. His desire, however, soon turned to arrogance. He grasped Vedavati's hair, intent on claiming her.

But Vedavati, infused with divine power, magically freed herself. Her eyes blazed with a fierce determination.

'With my dying words, I curse you, Dashagreeva!' she exclaimed, her voice echoing through the forest. 'I will be born again, and my rebirth will seal your destruction.'

With those words, Vedavati cast herself into the flames, her spirit ascending to the heavens. Vedavati's soul would reincarnate as Sita, the future queen of Ayodhya, and the wife of Rama, the hero destined to vanquish Dashagreeva.

The gods themselves ordained Vedavati's rebirth, weaving a tapestry of fate that would entwine Dashagreeva, Rama, and Sita in an epic struggle between good and evil.

Under the moonlit canopy of another forest, Dashagreeva, the mighty king of Lanka, chanced upon Rambha, the enchanting Queen of the Apsaras. Her ethereal beauty mesmerised him, and his desires flared like a wildfire.

Rambha, wife of Nalakuvara, Kubera's son, wandered lost in thought, unaware of the danger lurking nearby. Dashagreeva's eyes devoured her, and his lust consumed him.

With brazen audacity, Dashagreeva seized Rambha, his whispers dripping with malice. 'How fortunate for you that we have met!'

Rambha's shock turned to outrage as she struggled against his grasp. 'Release me!' she cried. 'You are my elder relative, my uncle-in-law! My husband Nalakuvara is your nephew. Let me go!'

But Dashagreeva knew no shame. He ignored the bonds of kinship and brutally violated Rambha, shattering her dignity and trust.

The aftermath of that fateful night found Rambha before Nalakuvara, her tears and anguish pouring forth as she recounted Dashagreeva's transgression.

Nalakuvara's wrath ignited, and he unleashed a curse upon his step-uncle. 'If Dashagreeva ever touches another woman against her will, his head will split into a thousand pieces.'

Thus, the seeds of Dashagreeva's downfall were sown. His reckless disregard for the sacred bonds of family and his blatant disrespect for women's autonomy would ultimately prove to be his undoing.

Dashagreeva returned to Lanka to continue his reign, fuelled by his unbridled arrogance and lust, blissfully unaware of the destruction that the curses of Anaranya, Vedavati and Nalakuvara would wreak on his life.

SIXTEEN

The Terrifying Shriek

Under Shiva's Toe

Dashagreeva, determined to expand his dominion, vowed to conquer Yama, the God of Death. He rode his chariot south towards the Land of the Dead, leaving Lanka's shores behind. Yama's soldiers, steadfast in their duty, attacked Dashagreeva. But the mighty king of Lanka destroyed them all.

Yama himself then rode forth to face Dashagreeva. The God of Death's presence struck fear into the hearts of Dashagreeva's soldiers, and they fled in terror. Alone on the battlefield, Dashagreeva and Yama clashed. Their fierce battle raged for seven days and nights, shaking the foundations of the underworld.

Yama prepared to strike Dashagreeva with his Death-Hammer, *Kaladanda,* but just as Yama was about to deliver the fatal blow, Brahma, the Creator, appeared on the battlefield.

'Halt!' Brahma spoke. 'I gave Dashagreeva my blessing; no Deva can kill him, not even the God of Death.'

Yama hesitated, his duty conflicting with Brahma's words. Brahma reassured Yama, 'Lord Vishnu will incarnate as a human to annihilate Dashagreeva and the demon clan.'

Yama nodded, withdrawing his *Kaladanda.* Dashagreeva, though battered, stood tall, his life spared. With Brahma's words, the battle ceased. Yama vanished. Dashagreeva declared himself Conqueror of Death, his arrogance swelling. 'I have conquered the God of Death himself,' Dashagreeva boasted. 'No one can stand against me.'

But Brahma's prophecy lingered, a reminder of Dashagreeva's eventual downfall.

One day, Dashagreeva found himself journeying through the streets of Ashma. A magnificent palace, whose splendour rivalled the heights of Mount Meru, loomed ahead. The grand house, with its pearl-adorned walls, golden pillars, and crystalline staircases, seemed to pulse with an otherworldly energy.

Curious to know who resided in such splendour, he ordered his trusted general, Prahasta, to investigate. Obeying the command, Prahasta ventured deep into the palace, moving from chamber to chamber. Each room was grander than the last, yet unnervingly empty. Finally, in the seventh chamber, he encountered a strange sight—a flame flickering in the corner of the room. Within the flame, two figures emerged, one laughing eerily and the other garlanded with golden lotuses, his presence radiant and fearsome like the blazing sun. Prahasta, overcome by the power of the scene, quickly returned to his lord and described what he had seen.

Unshaken, Dashagreeva descended from his celestial

chariot, his face set in determination. The air around him darkened as he strode toward the palace. But before he could enter, a figure blocked his path—a colossal, terrifying being with a flaming tongue and eyes burning red. In his hand, he carried an iron mace, and his form seemed to radiate pure dread. Even Dashagreeva, fearless as he was, felt a shiver run down his spine. Yet, swallowing his apprehension, he faced the figure.

'What brings you here, O lord of Rakshasas?' the guardian asked in a booming voice. 'Do you seek battle, or is there another reason for your visit?'

Dashagreeva's mind raced, but his voice remained steady. 'Who resides within this house?' he asked, refusing to be intimidated. 'I seek to challenge the one who would dare oppose me.'

The guardian, his fiery eyes gleaming, answered, 'This house belongs to Bali, the lord of the Danavas. He is a being of immense strength, a protector of truth, and invincible in battle. Be warned, O king of Rakshasas, for Bali is not easily defeated.'

Despite the ominous warning, Dashagreeva pressed forward. He was no stranger to threats, and he had faced powerful enemies before. As he entered the grand hall, the figure of Bali came into view—a towering presence, his eyes gleaming like molten gold, his laughter reverberating through the palace walls.

'O lord of Lanka,' Bali greeted him, his voice deep and commanding. 'What brings you to my domain? Do you seek knowledge or a challenge?'

Dashagreeva's response was blunt and filled with pride. 'I have heard tales of your imprisonment by

Vishnu,' he said, his eyes narrowing. 'If you wish, I can release you from those bonds. I am capable of freeing you from any curse or constraint.'

Bali's laughter grew louder, filling the hall with an unsettling echo. 'You are mistaken, Dashagreeva,' he said, his voice tinged with both amusement and wisdom. 'It was not Vishnu who bound me, but the very force of Time itself. The figure who stands at my door is not a mere guardian but the embodiment of Time, the destroyer and creator of all things. No one, not even I, can escape his grasp. He is both Death and Life, and his power governs the fate of all beings, including you.'

Dashagreeva's brow furrowed, his pride stung by Bali's words. 'I do not fear Time,' he declared. 'I have faced many foes, and I will not be cowed by such tales.'

Bali's eyes softened as he regarded the lord of Lanka. 'You do not understand the true nature of the forces you are dealing with,' he said quietly. 'Time spares no one—not even the greatest of warriors. I have seen mighty beings fall before its power. The likes of Vritra, Kalanemi, and even my own ancestors have been brought low by Time's inexorable march. Even now, you stand before its gaze, though you may not realise it.'

He gestured towards a massive disc-shaped ornament that lay near them, glowing with an intense golden light. 'Do you see that ornament? Take it up and bring it to me,' Bali commanded. 'Do not delay, O King of Lanka.'

With a laugh, the lord of Lanka strode towards the glowing piece of jewellery, his pride swelling within him. He reached down and grasped the ornament with his powerful arms. Dashagreeva, still filled with self-assurance, attempted to lift it. However, to his surprise and growing frustration, the celestial object refused to budge. Its immense weight defied his efforts, as if rooted to the very core of the earth. He was known for lifting mountains and uprooting mighty trees, yet this jewel would not yield to his strength.

Shocked and embarrassed, Dashagreeva's confidence wavered. Not one to accept defeat easily, he tried again, this time with all his might. His muscles tensed, his face reddened with strain, but the *kundala* remained unmoved. Suddenly, the effort proved too great, and Dashagreeva collapsed to the ground, blood pouring from his mouth and nostrils due to the exertion of immense force. The pride of Lanka lay battered on the ground, bloodied and broken.

Yet Dashagreeva, being no ordinary warrior, quickly regained his senses. He rose, though his spirit was bruised, and he lowered his head before Bali. His arrogance, at least for the moment, had been curbed by the sheer weight of the relic of a time far beyond his comprehension.

Bali, seeing Dashagreeva's struggle, spoke again, but this time with a tone of understanding, mingled with a hint of pity. 'Come close, O foremost of Rakshasas, and listen to my words,' he said. 'The *kundala* you tried to lift is no ordinary jewel. It is an ornament that belonged to my ancestor, Hiranyakashipu, a being of such immense power that neither Time, Death, nor illness could touch him. His death could not come in the day, nor at night; not by weapon, not by human, god, or animal. And yet,

Narasimha—a figure that was neither man nor beast—slew Hiranyakashipu with his bare hands, bypassing the blessings and protections the Danava king had so carefully obtained. The figure who destroyed Hiranyakashipu is none other than Narayana, the supreme Lord, standing guard at the entrance to my palace.'

'This *kundala*, crested with jewels, fell during Hiranyakashipu's battle with Narasimha. It is a relic of his might, but also a reminder that no power in the universe, no matter how strong, can defy the inexorable march of Time.'

Bali's words were not merely a recounting of history but a lesson—a warning to Dashagreeva that his might, though great, had its limits in the grand scheme of the universe. The *kundala*, representing both the glory and downfall of Hiranyakashipu, was beyond the power of Dashagreeva, a reminder that some forces could not be overcome by strength alone.

Dashagreeva, wounded in pride, struggled to regain his composure. Bali continued, 'Do you see now, Dashagreeva? Even you, with all your strength, are but a speck in the vast currents of Time. No force in this creation can escape Time or the will of the gods.'

Dashagreeva could feel the weight of Bali's words pressing down on him, but still, he refused to yield. 'I am not defeated,' he growled. 'I will not be bound by the limits of gods or fate.'

Bali sighed. 'You have much to learn, lord of Lanka,' he said. 'Perhaps in time, you will understand the true nature of power and its limits. But for now, go. Seek your answers elsewhere.'

With his head held high, despite the shame burning in his chest, Dashagreeva turned and left the palace. Even as the weight of Bali's words settled deep within him, his pride refused to be extinguished. One day, he would prove that even Time could be conquered.

In the sacred land of Bharata, King Marutta prepared for a grand sacrifice. The Devas, including Indra, Yama, Kubera, and Varuna attended the ritual, alongside esteemed priests.

However, the tranquillity was shattered by Dashagreeva's arrival. The mighty king of Lanka appeared, his Rakshasa powers stoking an air of fear. The Devas, sensing danger, disguised themselves as animals. Indra transformed into a peacock, Yama into a crow, Kubera into a lizard, and Varuna into a swan.

Dashagreeva, undeterred, challenged Marutta to a fight. The priests, recognising the futility of resistance, advised the king to surrender.

'I have won!' Dashagreeva declared, his voice thundering across the landscape. He then killed the priests, drank their blood, and flew away, leaving devastation in his wake.

The Devas, relieved at their narrow escape, bestowed blessings upon the animals whose disguises had protected them from Dashagreeva's wrath.

Kubera, appalled by Dashagreeva's repeated atrocities against priests, Devas, and Yakshas, sent a message to his half-brother. 'Your deeds dishonour our father,' the messenger urged. 'Cease your destructive path.'

Enraged, Dashagreeva slaughtered the messenger

and vowed to destroy Kubera and the world's guardians. 'None dare speak to Dashagreeva thus!' he roared, rallying his Rakshasa army.

Dashagreeva's forces assaulted Kubera's Himalayan stronghold Alaka. Kubera rallied his Yaksha warriors, but they were no match for the Rakshasas.

The battlefield transformed into a gruesome landscape of carnage, with Yaksha corpses strewn across the snow-covered mountains.

Kubera, gravely wounded, confronted Dashagreeva. 'Your actions will bring ruin upon you,' Kubera warned. 'One day, someone will send you to the depths of hell.'

The half-brothers clashed; their powers locked in a fierce struggle. Dashagreeva emerged victorious, claiming Kubera's *Pushpaka Vimana* as spoils. Triumphant, he turned towards Lanka.

Dashagreeva flew back to his kingdom on the *Pushpaka Vimana*, Kubera's flying chariot. As he soared through the skies, he encountered a dense mountain forest. Nandi, Shiva's divine bull, cautioned Dashagreeva against disturbing the sacred site. 'Turn back, Dashagreeva! This is Shiva's realm.'

Dashagreeva, swollen with pride over his strength and conquests, sought to demonstrate his might by attempting to lift Mount Kailash itself, causing tremors that shook the universe.

Parvati and Shiva, dwelling on Mount Kailash, were disturbed. Parvati sought refuge in Shiva's embrace. Shiva playfully pressed the mountain with his toe, trapping

Dashagreeva beneath the mountain.

Dashagreeva let out a terrifying shriek which reverberated across the cosmos, shaking heaven, earth, and the underworld.

For many years, Dashagreeva remained trapped. Terrified sages advised Dashagreeva to seek Shiva's forgiveness. 'Humble yourself before the Great God, lest catastrophe befall you.' Dashagreeva heeded their counsel. He composed and sang hymns in praise of Shiva for a thousand years.

Pleased by Dashagreeva's persistence and devotion, Shiva eventually relented, releasing him from the mountain's confines.

'What is it that you seek?' Shiva asked, his voice as deep and resonant as the cosmos itself.

Dashagreeva looked up at the great god. 'Lord, I seek your blessings. Grant me your strength and protection, for then, no force in the universe will be able to stand against me.'

'Your name shall be Ravana,' Shiva declared. The name 'Ra-Vana' emerged from the terrifying cry that shook the universe. 'For your scream of agony echoed throughout the three worlds, instilling fear. From now on, deities, humans, Yakshas, and all earthly inhabitants shall recognise you as Ravana—the terror of creatures.'

Ravana's encounter with Shiva ignited a fire within him. His ambition to conquer the three worlds burned brighter. Ravana's fate, entwined with the cosmos, would soon unfold.

Shiva smiled, pleased with Ravana's devotion. 'You are already invincible, Ravana,' he said, using the name that would henceforth define him. 'But I will grant you a boon—my sword, the *Chandrahasa*, a weapon of immense power.'

Shiva placed the divine sword, its blade glowing with an ethereal light, in Ravana's hands.

'Use it wisely.' Shiva said.

Ravana, overcome with gratitude, accepted the sword with reverence. From that day forward, Ravana was known as the greatest devotee of Shiva, and his worship of Shiva made his power grow beyond measure.

Ravana's ambition, coupled with his newfound invincibility, began to warp his mind. With the sword of Shiva in his hand and the boons of Brahma protecting him, Ravana now became truly unstoppable. The lessons of his father Vishrava, who had once taught him the ways of dharma and restraint, were slowly being drowned out by an insatiable appetite for power and the urge for conquests. The city of Lanka, now fully under his control, was only the beginning. The world lay before him, ripe for the taking.

Sumali, wise and venerable, sought to temper Ravana's fiery nature. 'My grandson,' he said, 'your creativity knows no bounds. Yet, I worry about the turmoil that often accompanies your passion. Can you harness your emotions, or will they consume you?'

Ravana's gaze faltered, 'The fire within me burns brighter with each passing day. Sometimes, I fear it will engulf me.'

Sumali's expression turned sombre. 'The line between brilliance and madness is thin, Ravana. Tread carefully, lest your genius become your downfall.'

Ravana's brow furrowed, sceptical. 'How can these pursuits tame my inner storms?'

Sumali smiled. 'The harmony of the universe lies within the arts. Discover their secrets, and you shall find balance.'

Intrigued, Ravana thus began his explorations. Often, he sat amidst a scatter of strings and woods tinkering with experimental instruments. Sumali observed with interest as Ravana's fingers moved deftly, testing the resonance of his new creations. As Ravana practised, his music became a bridge to Shiva's realm.

'Grandfather, my instrument will capture the essence of Shiva's cosmic dance.'

Days turned into weeks as Ravana refined his invention. The *Rudra Veena* took shape, its tones echoing the divine harmonies of the universe.

Ravana's days blurred into a maelstrom of administrative duties, strategic alliances, and philosophical contemplation. His nights, however, belonged to his art. The *Rudra Veena*, his masterly creation, beckoned, its melodies echoing the turmoil within.

In the stillness of his chambers, Ravana's fingers danced upon the *Rudra Veena's* strings, conjuring harmonies that transcended mortal bounds. His music became an extension of his soul, a reflection of the cosmic dance he sought to understand.

As the days passed, Ravana's creativity surged. His poetry, infused with the rhythms of the *Rudra Veena*, captured the essence of Shiva's destructive and creative power. Yet, beneath the surface of his creative fervour, Ravana's emotions seethed. The darkness that had long lurked within him began to stir once more, fed by the intensity of his art.

He desperately needed an anchor.

Ravana sought strategic alliances through marriage, solidifying his power. He went on to marry Mandodari, Mayasura's beautiful daughter, and Dhanyamalini, a skilled warrior-princess.

Mandodari's gentle nature went far beyond an alliance of convenience. She soothed Ravana's turbulent soul. Yet, Ravana's emotions continued to simmer, threatening to boil over.

'Mandodari,' Ravana whispered to his queen, 'I feel the shadows gathering, the winds of chaos howling through my mind.'

Mandodari's soothing touch calmed him. 'Your genius is a double-edged sword, my lord. It cuts through the veil of reality, but also threatens to consume you.'

Ravana's gaze locked onto hers, his eyes burning. 'I will not be swayed. I will harness this… this storm.'

Mandodari wordlessly held him close to her heart, as Sumali's words echoed in Ravana's mind, 'The line between brilliance and madness is thin.'

Ravana's struggles to tame his emotions had only just begun.

'Before reincarnating as Dantavakra, long after having lived as Hiranyaksha, in this present life, my beloved brother Vijaya was born as my sibling, Kumbhakarna. He has gone back to Vaikuntha before me, redeemed of the terrible curse of the Sanatkumaras. Kumbhakarna's loyalty was as immense as his form, his strength unparalleled. Cursed with insatiable sleep, he fought beside me only in times of dire need, his heart pure despite his monstrous form. He fought valiantly against the forces of Rama, but even his immense power could not alter the fate woven by the divine. Our hubris led us to challenge the gods, and Kumbhakarna's loyalty could not save us from the repercussions of our defiance. His fall, like mine, is a testament to the limits of even the greatest might and the inevitable consequences of challenging the divine.

'Remember my tale, mortals: loyalty and strength are virtues, but they cannot override the cosmic order. Balance and humility are the true paths to lasting greatness.'

–Ravana, Emperor of Lanka

SEVENTEEN

Kumbhakarna

Shadows of Lanka

The sun dipped low over the vast city of Lanka as Kumbhakarna stood at the edge of the city, a solitary figure silhouetted against the dying light. The weight of his existence felt heavier than ever, burdened by a hunger that reached beyond mere sustenance—a yearning for peace, for understanding, in a world that demanded bloodshed.

His early years had been a whirlwind of power and conflict. From the moment he took his first steps, the ground trembled with the force of his strides, each movement a testament to his unyielding strength. He was born with the might of a thousand elephants, yet what good was such power when it could not quell the turmoil within?

As he reflected on the path that had brought him here, Kumbhakarna's thoughts drifted to his elder brother. He often found himself at odds with Ravana. Where Ravana hungered for power and dominion over the gods themselves, Kumbhakarna felt a weariness with such pursuits. His victories, though glorious and celebrated by his kin, had left him empty. He did not revel in the bloodshed, nor did he take joy in the conquest. He had long stopped finding meaning in these things, unlike Ravana, who seemed to thrive on the terror he inspired.

'Kumbhakarna,' Ravana had once said, his voice sharp and commanding as they stood in the halls of Lanka's great palace, 'The gods themselves tremble at the mention of your name. Yama, Indra, even the creator Brahma—they cower when you step onto the battlefield. Why, then, do you linger here? Why do you refuse to join me in bringing the heavens to their knees?'

Kumbhakarna had looked at his brother, his eyes heavy with a weariness Ravana could never understand. 'Is there no end to the wars, brother? Must we always fight, always hunger for more? What peace is there in ruling the heavens if we destroy everything in our path to get there?'

Ravana had laughed, a sound that sent chills through the room. 'Peace is for the weak! You are the strongest being in the universe. Why not embrace your destiny?'

Kumbhakarna had shaken his head, the disappointment evident in his gaze. 'Strength without purpose is a curse, not a blessing.'

The shadows deepened as he recalled his brother's ambition, the fires of conquest that burned within him. Kumbhakarna's victories, celebrated by his kin, only left him feeling hollow. He had grown weary of the endless battles, the bloodshed that seemed to consume his world. Yet, there was a time when he had been driven by the same ferocity that now characterised his elder brother. His rage had once been unbridled. In his youth, he had devastated Indra's sacred Nandana Garden, leaving a trail of destruction in his wake. Seven apsaras fell by his hand, along with ten of Indra's devoted followers. In the aftermath, he roamed the divine grounds, unrepentant, as the scent of crushed blossoms mingled with the blood he had spilled. It was a savage victory that summoned Indra's fury, and soon the king of the gods arrived, riding his majestic Airavata.

'Your savagery ends here!' Indra had bellowed, the thunderbolt, Vajra, gleaming in his hand.

Kumbhakarna had stood firm, unyielding as the mountain, and when Indra hurled the Vajra at him, the impact sent shockwaves through the battlefield. He could still feel the moment when the bolt struck him—a fleeting pain, a mere scratch against the might of his being. He remembered looking down, the mark left behind insignificant against the vastness of his power.

'Is this all the might of the heavens?' he had challenged, his voice rumbling like distant thunder.

In that moment, he had seized the tusk of Airavata, wrenching it free and hurling it back at Indra. The blow had sent the king of the gods tumbling to the ground, his divine armour shattered, his pride in tatters. Yet Kumbhakarna had chosen not to deliver the final blow, letting Indra flee instead.

It was a memory Kumbhakarna could never erase—a testament to his strength, but also to the violence that once defined him. That battle, though a testament to his overwhelming strength, had left Kumbhakarna empty, much like his victories over Yama and other gods. The momentary triumph, the thrill of battle—it all paled in comparison to the hollow feeling that followed.

'Why do you not finish what you started?' his brother had demanded after the battle, anger flaring in his eyes.

'Because I do not wish to be known as a destroyer,' Kumbhakarna had replied. 'What is the point of such victory if it leaves me feeling emptier than before?'

That emptiness weighed heavily on him, a burden he could not shake. Ravana could never understand this. For him, power was everything. But for Kumbhakarna, it was nothing without purpose.

Then there had been Yama, the god of death himself. That battle had been different. Where Indra had fought with fury and pride, Yama had faced Kumbhakarna with a quiet, solemn respect. The lord of death had stood before him, weapon in hand, his dark eyes gazing into Kumbhakarna's soul.

'You are a rare being,' Yama had said, his voice a deep rumble. 'Even I cannot claim you. There is no place for you in the realms of the dead, Kumbhakarna. Your strength is beyond death itself.'

Kumbhakarna had said nothing, but his heart had stirred at Yama's words. He had not fought to kill Yama, nor had Yama sought to end him. There had been no victor, only an unspoken understanding between them—a recognition that Kumbhakarna was not of this world or the next. He was something beyond the cycle of life and death, a force that could not be tamed or destroyed.

But that knowledge brought him no comfort. If anything, it only deepened the void inside him. He often sought solace beneath the ancient banyan tree outside the palace, its expansive branches providing shade from the relentless sun. It was a place where he could reflect on his choices, the lives he had taken, and the insatiable hunger that gnawed at his spirit.

On one such day, as he sat in silence, his wife Vajrajvala approached. Her presence was like a balm to his troubled heart. Despite her own formidable strength, she carried a gentleness that drew him in, a counterbalance to the turmoil that surrounded him.

'Dearest husband,' she said softly, settling beside him. 'You carry too much weight. You cannot bear the burden of the world alone.'

He sighed, looking away from her piercing gaze. 'I do not know how to put it down. I do not know how to find peace.'

Vajrajvala placed a comforting hand on his arm, her touch grounding him. 'Perhaps peace is not something we find. Perhaps it is something we create together.'

Her words lingered in his mind, offering a glimmer of hope amidst the shadows. But the call of battle was ever-present. Ravana would summon him again, as he always did, to lead their armies against the celestial beings who opposed them. Each time, Kumbhakarna rose, not from desire but from a sense of obligation—to his brother, to his family, to the legacy they were building.

And so, the cycle continued. His heart ached as he fought, each clash of steel and roar of battle fuelling his discontent. The gods fell before him, but with each victory, he found no solace—only a deeper yearning for understanding.

In the quiet of night, after a day of fierce combat, Kumbhakarna would return to his family, their laughter ringing like music in his ears. Kumbha and Nikumbha, his sons, played at his feet, their innocence a stark contrast to the bloodshed that marked their father's existence. He would watch them, marvelling at their joy, and yet, a part of him feared for their future.

'Father,' Kumbha would say, his eyes wide with admiration, 'tell us of your battles! Did you defeat the gods?'

Kumbhakarna would look down at his sons, his heart swelling with pride and sorrow. 'Yes, my son,' he would say, his voice low. 'But victories come at a cost.'

'Why do you fight if it makes you sad?' Nikumbha would ask, his innocence piercing through the darkness that clouded Kumbhakarna's heart.

A question he had often asked himself, one he could not answer. 'I fight to protect you,' he would respond, but the truth was more complex, tangled in the web of his own conflicting desires.

Days turned to weeks, and the battles continued, each one more intense than the last. The gods began to fear Kumbhakarna, and whispers reached even the ears of Brahma, the creator. They spoke of a force beyond reckoning, a being whose hunger for knowledge and understanding threatened to consume the very fabric of existence. Kumbhakarna was not merely a warrior; he was a titan, an enigma.

One evening, as twilight descended, Brahma gathered the gods in a celestial council. The air was thick with tension, each deity acutely aware of Kumbhakarna's growing power.

'His strength is unparalleled,' said Indra, still nursing

the wounds of his humiliation. 'We cannot allow him to roam free. He poses a threat to the very order of the universe.'

'But what can we do?' Yama countered, his deep voice resonating with a solemnity that filled the chamber. 'I faced him and could not bind him. He is a force of nature.'

'Perhaps we must approach him differently,' suggested Saraswati, the goddess of wisdom. 'Instead of confronting him with brute force, we might seek to understand him. Kumbhakarna yearns for knowledge, and perhaps we can appeal to that hunger.'

Brahma pondered her words, feeling the weight of the decision before him. 'Very well. I will approach him, but we must tread carefully. He is not a being to be underestimated.'

As the council dispersed, Kumbhakarna remained unaware of the celestial deliberations. Despite his indomitable might, he had always felt out of place in a world that celebrated his power yet offered no solace for the deeper questions that gnawed at him. It was during such moments of reflection that Kumbhakarna had come to the realisation that his strength alone would not grant him the peace he longed for. He had retreated to the banyan tree once more, seeking the solace it provided. The gentle rustle of leaves surrounded him, and he closed his eyes, breathing deeply. In that moment, he felt a presence—one unlike any other.

'Who dares approach me?' Kumbhakarna called, his voice resonating through the night.

From the shadows stepped Brahma, The Creator, his

aura a blend of divine light and wisdom. Kumbhakarna opened his eyes, surprise washing over him.

'Brahmadev,' he said, lowering his guard. 'What brings you to the realm of mortals?'

The Creator regarded him with a gaze that held centuries of knowledge. 'I have come to speak with you, Kumbhakarna. I seek to understand the depths of your hunger.'

Kumbhakarna's brow furrowed in confusion. 'You wish to understand me? I am a demon—a force of chaos. What is there to understand?'

Brahma smiled gently, the corners of his eyes crinkling. 'You are much more than that. You possess strength unmatched, yet you yearn for something beyond mere power. Tell me, what is it you seek?'

For the first time, Kumbhakarna felt the weight of his burdens ease slightly. 'I seek understanding, Brahmadev. I long to know why I was given such power when all it brings is conflict. I do not desire to be a monster, yet the world sees me as one.'

Brahma nodded, understanding dawning in his eyes. 'The world often misinterprets strength as a lack of compassion. You fight not for conquest but for the hope of peace, do you not?'

Kumbhakarna's heart stirred at the truth of those words. 'Yes, but every victory leaves me feeling emptier. I do not find joy in battle, only an unquenchable hunger for meaning.'

Brahma stepped closer, his presence radiating warmth. 'Then let us find that meaning together. You are not bound by the expectations of others. You have the power to forge your own destiny.'

As they spoke, the shadows around them seemed to shift, a dance of light and darkness interwoven in the air. Kumbhakarna felt a flicker of hope—a possibility that perhaps peace could be achieved without bloodshed, that his strength could be a force for creation, not destruction.

'Will you guide me, great-grandfather?' Kumbhakarna asked, vulnerability seeping into his voice. 'Will you help me understand the true nature of my existence?'

Brahma extended a hand, a gesture of solidarity. 'Together, we will seek the truth. You have the power to reshape the world, Kumbhakarna. Turn your hunger into something that nurtures rather than consumes.'

Brahma advised him to seek out the wisdom of his grand-uncle Narada, a sage known not only for his knowledge of the cosmos but for his deep understanding of the soul's journey.

Soon, Kumbhakarna stood at the entrance of the tranquil grove where Narada, the divine sage, sat, strumming his *veena* with an effortless grace. The melody wafted through the air, beckoning Kumbhakarna closer. As he reached the sage, Narada looked up, his eyes sparkling with wisdom.

'Kumbhakarna, mighty Rakshasa,' Narada said, his voice warm and inviting. 'You come seeking knowledge. What weighs on your heart?'

'I seek to understand my purpose beyond my strength, great sage,' Kumbhakarna replied. 'I wish to find meaning in my existence.'

Narada nodded, gesturing for him to sit. 'Listen closely, for I shall share the essence of wisdom.'

Kumbhakarna sat down, 'I am ready.'

'Know thyself,' Narada began, his voice steady. 'For within you lies the seed of all understanding.'

'Strength without purpose is but a shadow,' he continued. 'Wield it wisely, or it will consume you.'

Kumbhakarna pondered these words. 'I have fought many battles, yet they leave me feeling empty.'

'The true warrior fights for justice, not for glory,' Narada advised. 'Seek to protect, not to conquer.'

'Compassion is the mightiest weapon,' the sage added. 'When you uplift others, you rise above your own burdens.'

'Listen more than you speak,' Narada said, his gaze penetrating. 'Every heart has a story; understanding begins with listening.'

'Embrace vulnerability,' he continued. 'To show your wounds is to reveal your strength.'

'In service to others, you find yourself,' Narada advised. 'The joy of giving nourishes the soul.'

Kumbhakarna spoke softly. 'I wish to protect my family and my kingdom.'

'Lead with humility,' Narada reminded him. 'A true leader walks beside their people, not above them.'

'Your strength can be a shield,' he continued. 'But remember, it must also be a bridge to understanding.'

'Reflect often,' Narada urged. 'In stillness, the mind reveals its truths.'

'You are not merely your strength or your battles,' he added, his voice echoing wisdom. 'You are the sum of your choices.'

Kumbhakarna felt the words resonating deep within his core. 'But what if I fail?'

'Failure is the beginning of wisdom,' Narada reassured him. 'Each stumble is a step toward growth.'

'Do not fear the shadows of your past,' he continued. 'They are merely guides leading you to the light.'

'In every moment lies a choice,' Narada stated, his eyes unwavering. 'Choose love over fear, and your path will illuminate.'

'Remember, the journey is long,' Narada advised. 'Be patient with yourself as you walk the path of self-discovery.'

Kumbhakarna bowed deeply to Narada. 'Thank you for your guidance, sage. I shall strive to embody these teachings and share them with my family and my kingdom.'

'Go forth, Kumbhakarna,' Narada said, a smile gracing his lips. 'Embrace your journey with courage and love.'

In the days that followed, Kumbhakarna began to explore this new path. He sought out sages, scholars, and those who possessed knowledge of the universe. He travelled to distant lands, learning from wise beings who had witnessed the rise and fall of empires. With each lesson, he felt the burdens of his past begin to lighten, the endless hunger for understanding transforming into a quest for wisdom.

And yet, as Kumbhakarna grew in knowledge, Ravana's ambitions did not wane. The call to battle still echoed in the chambers of Lanka, and his brother, ever the conqueror, sought to draw Kumbhakarna back into the fray.

'Kumbhakarna!' Ravana roared one evening, storming into the great hall where Kumbhakarna was studying ancient texts. 'The gods gather once more! They plot against us! We must act!'

Kumbhakarna looked up from his scrolls, his heart heavy with the knowledge he had gained. 'And what good will another battle do, brother? What will it prove?'

'Power!' Ravana shouted, his voice ringing with fervour. 'We must show them our might. You, above all, are our greatest weapon!'

'Power without purpose is a trap, Ravana,' Kumbhakarna countered, his voice steady. 'I will not be a part of this cycle of destruction any longer.'

His brother's eyes darkened with anger. 'You are a fool! The world respects strength. It fears you. Embrace it!'

Kumbhakarna stood firm, the weight of his brother's words echoing in the chamber. 'Fear is not respect. I will no longer be a source of terror. I choose a different path.'

Ravana sneered, his anger boiling over. 'Then you are no brother of mine! You forsake your heritage and your strength for this foolish notion of peace!'

With that, he stormed out. The battle between the brothers had reached a boiling point, and Kumbhakarna felt a profound sadness settle within him. His desire for understanding had driven a wedge between them, but he could not turn back.

'And now, mortals and gods who witness my fall, as Ravana, whose intellect and power were unmatched, I lie dying on the battlefield.

'I mastered the Vedas, conquered realms, and sought to make Lanka a paradise. Yet, my pride and desire for dominance led me to abduct Sita, challenging the very gods. My actions brought ruin upon my kingdom, the death of my kin, and the fall of my empire.

'My brother Vibhishana's betrayal and my own defiance against Rama sealed my fate. As the divine arrows pierce my navel, where my life force resides, I see the folly of my ways. Power, without humility and wisdom, leads to downfall. My story is a warning: the greatest enemy lies within, and unchecked ambition brings only destruction.

'Let my life and death be a lesson that true strength lies in understanding and respecting the divine order. In my final moments, I relinquish my pride, embracing the peace that eluded me, hoping that others may learn from my mistakes.'

–Ravana, Emperor of Lanka

EIGHTEEN

Minakshi and Vidyutjihva

The End Begins

Beneath the pale moonlight Lanka's dark towers and fortresses stood as ominous sentinels against the horizon. Ravana, the great king of the Rakshasas, brooded as his mind churned in turmoil. The betrayal by Minakshi, his beloved sister, weighed heavily upon him. He had always been her protector, her guide, but Minakshi had chosen another path—a path that led her into the arms of their sworn enemies.

She had fallen in love with Vidyutjihva, a prince of the Kalakeya Danavas, whose tribe had long been a thorn in Ravana's side. Their treacherous ways were an insult to his dominion over the Three Worlds. The Kalakeyas had fought his people time and time again, their hatred for the Rakshasas like a festering wound. And yet, Minakshi, his only sister, had bound herself to them.

Ravana's fingers curled into fists as the memory of her departure came rushing back to him. He had pleaded with her not to go, had warned her that Vidyutjihva was no more than a serpent, his affection a ploy. But Minakshi's heart was already lost to the Kalakeya prince. She had left Lanka behind, following Vidyutjihva to his city of

Ashma, far to the east where the mountains met the sea.

Even as the memories haunted him, he acknowledged the bitter twist of fate that brought him to this moment. Vidyutjihva, the snake, had dared to strike at him. In an act of treachery, the Kalakeyas had set a trap during their last raid on Indra's domains. The prince, who had fought by Ravana's side during their last attack upon Indra's domains, had led Ravana into an ambush as they returned victorious, hoping to end the mighty Rakshasa king. Ravana had only barely escaped with his life. Now, the time for retribution had come.

With eyes as hard as stone, Ravana summoned his most trusted emissary. 'Send word to Minakshi,' he commanded, his voice as cold as the winds from the northern mountains. 'Tell her I seek peace. I will come to her city, to her home, and I will speak with Vidyutjihva as kin.'

The messenger, pale and uncertain, did not dare question the king. He bowed low and departed into the night, leaving Ravana alone with his thoughts.

The city of Ashma lay nestled within jagged peaks, its grey walls blending with the barren rock. A city built by the Kalakeyas, it had none of the grandeur of Lanka, but its people prided themselves on their strength, on their ability to endure. Within the palace, Minakshi stood upon a high balcony, her gaze lost in the distance. Her heart ached with the weight of the choice she had made. She had turned her back on her family, on Ravana, for love—a love that had brought her here, far from the land of her birth.

Yet Vidyutjihva's hold over her had begun to feel like a shackle. His ambition was fierce, his hatred for the Rakshasas undying. He had never hidden it from her, never pretended otherwise. In their shared moments, his voice was filled with venom whenever he spoke of Ravana. Minakshi's heart clenched with each word, torn between the man she loved and the brother she had once adored.

As the pale dawn broke, the news came. A message from Ravana himself. He wished for peace, to meet Vidyutjihva at their palace, to let bygones be bygones.

Minakshi's heart fluttered with hope. Perhaps the time for hatred was over. Perhaps her brother and her husband could finally see beyond their enmity.

Vidyutjihva, however, had no such hopes. When Minakshi approached him, the prince's expression was as unreadable as the darkened sky before a storm.

'Ravana wishes for peace,' she said softly, her voice filled with the fragile hope of reconciliation. 'He is coming here, to Ashma.'

'Peace?' Vidyutjihva laughed bitterly. 'Your brother knows nothing of peace. He is a snake, Minakshi, and he comes here to coil around us, to strike when we are least prepared.'

'But he is my brother,' she protested. 'He would not harm me.'

'And yet he will destroy all that I have built,' Vidyutjihva snapped. His eyes gleamed with something dark, something dangerous. 'But no matter. Let him come. I will welcome him as a prince should. But if he believes for a moment that I will bend the knee to him, he is sorely mistaken.'

Minakshi could say nothing more. She could only watch as Vidyutjihva prepared for Ravana's arrival, the tension in the air growing thicker with each passing hour.

Minakshi had always felt trapped beneath the heavy shadow cast by her brother, Ravana. His dominance was like a cloak, suffocating her every desire, every thought that strayed from his commands. As children, there had been love between them, but as they grew older, Ravana's control became relentless. Minakshi had no say in her own life. He would bark orders, and she was expected to obey without question. Over the years, this silent oppression grew into a deep-rooted resentment. She wasn't just Ravana's sister, she was his subject, his pawn in the grand game he played against gods and men alike.

Her bitterness grew sharper when she found love, true love, in the form of Vidyutjihva, the Kalakeya prince. The Kalakeyas, sworn enemies of the Rakshasas, were a constant thorn in Ravana's side. How could she, a princess of Lanka, even think of marrying into their bloodline? Ravana had opposed her at every step, denying her even the chance to think for herself. 'You'll marry who I deem worthy,' he had told her in one of his quieter moments. His voice had not been raised, but the weight of his will had crushed her spirit, leaving her cold and bitter.

It had been Mandodari, Ravana's queen, who intervened on her behalf. Only through Mandodari's calm reasoning, her soft-spoken persuasion, had Ravana relented. Minakshi had finally married Vidyutjihva, her love. But the resentment toward her brother never faded; it only hardened, like iron slowly cooling in the furnace of her heart. Ravana could dominate kingdoms, armies, and even gods, but he could not touch the fierce love she held for her husband. Or so she thought.

The years passed, and the tension between Ravana and the Kalakeyas never truly abated. Despite Vidyutjihva's marriage to Minakshi, the enmity between their clans festered, lurking like a serpent coiled to strike. When Ravana had led his forces into Indra's domain, Vidyutjihva had stood at his side, fighting fiercely. Together, they had cut through Indra's armies, and for a brief moment, it seemed as though the Kalakeyas and Rakshasas could find common ground.

But Ravana's eyes, as ever, looked beyond the immediate victory, his mind always on the lookout for webs of cunning. On their return from the battle, the Kalakeyas revealed their treachery. They turned on Ravana, attempting to ambush him and bring him to his knees. Vidyutjihva had orchestrated the trap, aiding Ravana in battle only to plot his murder in the aftermath.

When Ravana realised the depth of the betrayal, his fury knew no bounds. Yet, cunning as always, he did not lash out in open battle. Instead, he sent a message to Minakshi, the sister who he knew harboured bitterness toward him. With his words, he softened the tension, extending a hand in what appeared to be peace. He claimed to have let go of past grievances, inviting her and Vidyutjihva to a meeting at the Kalakeya's palace.

Mandodari and Kumbhakarna had seen through Ravana's thin veil of civility. 'Do not kill him,' they had urged. Kumbhakarna, his great bulk hunched as he crouched beside his brother, his voice soft and full of concern, warned Ravana of the consequences of spilling Vidyutjihva's blood. 'Minakshi loves him. Do not take away her happiness for the sake of pride.'

Mandodari, ever the calm voice of reason in Ravana's tumultuous life, had joined in the plea. 'The Kalakeyas may be our enemies, but Vidyutjihva has fought by your side. Let not blood beget more blood. You've achieved victory already, my lord, why ruin it?'

Ravana had listened to them, or at least pretended to. He assured them that no harm would come to Vidyutjihva. But Ravana's mind was ever plotting, ever calculating. He had no intention of allowing the Kalakeya prince to walk free, not after such treachery. He devised a plan, knowing well the weaknesses of his foes.

The great hall of Vidyutjihva's palace was lit with the flickering glow of torches, their flames casting long shadows upon the stone walls. Ravana entered the hall alone, his towering form cutting a swathe through the cold air. His gaze fell upon Vidyutjihva, who stood at the far end of the chamber, Minakshi by his side.

'Sister,' Ravana greeted her, his voice like distant thunder. 'It has been too long.'

Minakshi stepped forward, her heart torn between joy and fear. 'Brother, I am glad you have come. I had hoped...'

Ravana's eyes softened as he looked at her. 'I am here for you, Minakshi. And for peace.' His gaze shifted to Vidyutjihva, hardening once more. 'Let us speak as brothers.'

Vidyutjihva inclined his head, his smile thin and sharp. 'Of course, Ravana. Let us speak.'

For a moment, the two warriors stared at each other, neither one willing to yield an inch. But then, with a suddenness that caught even Minakshi off guard, Ravana spoke again, his words sharp and biting.

'You Kalakeyas have always been cowards,' he said, his voice filled with contempt. 'You hide behind others, striking from the shadows, never daring to face your enemies openly. And you, Vidyutjihva, are no different.'

The room seemed to freeze. Vidyutjihva's face darkened, his hands trembling with barely contained rage. 'You come to my home, claiming peace, and then insult me?'

'I speak only the truth,' Ravana replied calmly. 'But if you cannot bear to hear it, perhaps you are weaker than I thought.'

That was all it took. With a roar of fury, Vidyutjihva lashed out, his tongue—a serpent's strike—wrapping around Ravana with the speed of lightning. Before anyone could react, the Kalakeya prince had engulfed the mighty Rakshasa king, swallowing him whole in a single, terrifying motion.

Minakshi screamed, her heart shattering as she watched her brother disappear. She turned to Vidyutjihva, her mind reeling. 'What have you done?' she cried, tears streaming down her face. 'You have killed him!'

Ravana had planned for this moment. Inside the dark belly of the Kalakeya prince, his strength had not faltered.

He had only to wait for Minakshi to make her choice.

The sound of Ravana's voice echoed from within Vidyutjihva's belly, calling out to Minakshi, commanding her. 'Sister, save me! Your husband, the man who claimed to love you, has turned against me. It is your blood, Minakshi, that is now called upon. Choose! Will you stand with your husband, or will you save your brother?'

Minakshi stood frozen in the middle of the grand hall, her mind torn asunder. She could feel the weight of the decision bearing down on her soul, crushing her beneath its terrible gravity. Vidyutjihva, the love of her life, stood before her, still as the storm that precedes the strike of lightning. Inside him, the brother who had controlled her entire life, who had driven her to resentment and rebellion, was now begging for her aid.

'Do not listen to him,' Vidyutjihva's voice came, sharp as the crack of thunder. 'He seeks to tear us apart, Minakshi. Let him perish, and we will be free of his shadow.'

But Minakshi's heart trembled. Blood called to blood. Could she allow her brother to die? Could she stand by and watch him be swallowed by the abyss of death?

With shaking hands, she gripped the dagger at her side. Slowly, painfully, she approached her husband, her mind writhing in turmoil. Vidyutjihva's eyes widened as the realisation dawned upon him.

'Minakshi,' he whispered, his voice laced with disbelief, 'what are you doing?'

Tears filled her eyes, blurring the edges of the world, as she raised the blade. In one swift motion, she drove it into Vidyutjihva's belly, cutting through flesh and bone, freeing Ravana from within. Blood sprayed across her, warm and thick, as her husband's body collapsed to the ground. And from within the gruesome wound, her brother emerged, alive and triumphant, crawling out like a dark creature from the bowels of the earth.

Minakshi staggered back, the horror of her actions crashing over her. She had killed the man she loved, and for what? For a brother who had never shown her anything but control and manipulation. The bitter taste of betrayal filled her mouth, and she turned her tear-streaked face to Ravana, her voice a broken whisper.

'You tricked me,' she choked, her words filled with hatred and sorrow. 'You knew I would choose you. You knew I would betray him.'

Ravana, standing tall once more, wiped the blood from his skin and looked at his sister with cold eyes. 'It was his fate,' he said simply. 'He was a threat to our people. He would have killed me, Minakshi. You saved your family.'

But Minakshi's heart was shattered beyond repair. She knelt beside the body of her husband, her sobs filling the empty hall. 'Could there be any brother,' she cried, her voice trembling with anguish, 'who would make his sister a widow? I acted in haste to save you from harm, without realising that you are invincible because of Brahma's boons! You played a terrible trick upon me! What brother would force this upon me, to choose between blood and love, only to lose everything?'

Ravana looked down at her, his expression softening just slightly. 'Minakshi, I cannot bring back Vidyutjihva. His fate was sealed the moment he raised his hand against me. But I give you my word that you will not remain alone. Whoever you choose next as your husband, I will see to it that he is yours. No one will deny you.'

His words, though meant to soothe, only deepened her grief. She rose slowly, her face pale and her eyes hollow. 'I will have no husband,' she said, her voice empty. 'You have taken from me the only man I will ever love.'

'Go now,' Ravana commanded, sensing her cold detachment. 'Take refuge with our cousin Khara. He will protect you, and with him are fourteen thousand Rakshasas who will serve you. Khara and Dushan will do as you bid.'

Without another word, Minakshi turned and walked away, leaving her brother standing amidst the blood and ruin of her heart. She did not look back. Her soul was too broken, too bitter, to ever forgive. The palace that had once been her home now felt like a prison, and she left it behind forever.

NINETEEN

Meghnada

The Weight of Legacy

Lanka glittered like a jewel under the midday sun, its golden spires reaching for the heavens. Ravana, lord of all Rakshasas, stood at the highest tower of his palace, his sharp gaze sweeping over his kingdom. To him, Lanka was more than a city; it was the culmination of his conquests, a monument to his unmatched power. Yet, deep within his heart, a shadow loomed.

His son, Meghnada.

Ravana's fingers gripped the stone balustrade, knuckles turning white. Meghnada was all he had ever desired in an heir—powerful, fearless, commanding the very elements themselves. Yet, as the boy grew into a man, there was something about him that unsettled the great king. Meghnada's victories no longer brought Ravana joy but an uneasy mixture of pride and envy.

He watched from his throne, applauded by his courtiers, as Meghnada returned victorious from another campaign. The Rakshasas hailed their prince with reverence, their voices rising in chants, 'Meghnada! The conqueror of the heavens! The Thunder Prince!'

A surge of pride swelled in Ravana's chest, but it was

quickly dampened by a gnawing sense of rivalry. They feared him, Ravana thought bitterly, eyes narrowing. But they loved his son. Ravana's own reputation—built over decades of war, bloodshed, and mastery of dark arts—now seemed fragile in the light of Meghnada's rising star. It gnawed at him. The Rakshasas had never cheered for him like this. Not with such affection.

Below, Meghnada dismounted from his chariot, his face obscured by his battle helm. His presence was commanding, a shadow of his father yet carved in a distinct mould. He radiated power, the air around him crackling faintly with a barely restrained storm.

Ravana descended the stairs slowly, purposefully, his long robes trailing behind him. When he approached his son, the court fell into a hushed silence. Their eyes met, and for a fleeting moment, something cold and primal flickered between them. Not love. Not hate. Something much more complicated.

'You fought well,' Ravana said, his voice a deep rumble, heavy with the weight of expectation. But his words felt hollow, even to himself.

'I fight as you taught me,' Meghnada responded, his tone respectful, yet there was a barely concealed edge beneath it—a yearning for something more.

Ravana studied his son. Meghnada had grown taller, broader, and there was an unmistakable confidence in his stance that set him apart from the nervous child he had once been. A confidence that bordered on arrogance.

'You fight as I command,' Ravana corrected, his eyes narrowing slightly. 'But power is not just in victory,

Meghnada. It is in control. You still have much to learn about that.'

Meghnada's jaw clenched. He knew this conversation well—the endless lectures, the lessons about restraint, discipline, control. But what his father failed to understand was that control came naturally to him. Power surged through his veins, unbidden. His mastery over the elements was second nature, not something to be leashed or tamed.

'I understand, Father,' he replied, though inside, his thoughts seethed with unspoken rebellion. Do you want me to remain a shadow forever? he wondered, his mind flickering with resentment. Will I always be an extension of your will?

The courtiers began to disperse, their eyes flicking nervously between the king and the prince. Though Ravana commanded their fear, it was Meghnada they admired, the young warrior with the strength to challenge the heavens. And Ravana could feel that admiration like a knife at his back.

As the halls emptied, Ravana placed a hand on his son's shoulder, squeezing harder than necessary. 'Come to my chambers tonight. We must discuss your future.'

Meghnada's lips twitched into a tight smile. 'Yes, Father.'

But the weight of that command sat heavily on him. My future. Or the one you have chosen for me?

The golden halls of Lanka glittered around him, but they felt more like a prison than a palace. Meghnada strode down the corridors, the sound of his boots echoing through the vast emptiness. He needed air. He needed escape from the suffocating aura of his father's expectations.

Without a second thought, he called upon his magic. His form shifted, his once regal armour fading into the simple garb of a commoner. His face morphed, his dark eyes dulling, his hair shortening, until he looked like any other man walking the streets of Lanka.

In these moments of anonymity, he found peace. The weight of his lineage fell away, and he could move unnoticed among his people—people who feared the throne but knew nothing of the man behind the crown.

As he strolled through the bustling marketplace, he felt something close to happiness. The vibrant colours, the hum of conversation, the scent of spiced meats and ripe fruits—all of it seemed more alive, more real, than the stifling grandeur of his father's court. Here, he was not a prince. He was not 'Indrajit, the conqueror of Indra.' He was simply a man.

But even in his anonymity, a small pang of loneliness crept in. He sought connection, friendship, but no matter where he turned, there was always a distance—created by fear of his father's wrath or awe of his own power.

That was, until he met Sulochana.

He had first seen her in the twilight just before dawn broke, at the abandoned Shiva temple on the coast. She came there every morning with her friends for her daily *puja* from her father Shesha's realm of Patala. He had watched her graceful movements from afar, as she made offerings to the *linga.* There was something about her—a strength, a quiet defiance that intrigued him. She didn't look at him with the fear he was used to seeing in others. Instead, her gaze was steady, questioning, as though she could see through his disguise and into the heart of him.

Over time, their meetings became frequent, secret. With her, he found freedom. Unlike everyone else in his life, Sulochana treated him as an equal, not a prince to be feared or a warrior to be revered. She saw him, Meghnada, not Ravana's son.

When he proposed marriage to her, it was one of the few decisions he had made on his own, without his father's intervention. For once, it was his choice, his path. And in that small act of rebellion, he found a taste of the independence he so desperately craved.

But even marriage could not shield him from the looming presence of his father.

That evening, as Meghnada returned to the palace, the weight of his father's words pressed heavily on his shoulders. Ravana had summoned him to discuss 'the future,' and Meghnada knew all too well what that meant.

The king sat in his chambers, the firelight casting long shadows across his face. His once sharp features had begun to soften with age, though the power in his eyes remained undiminished.

'You've proven yourself on the battlefield,' Ravana began without preamble. 'But your place is not yet secured. There are greater battles ahead, and you must be prepared.'

Meghnada listened in silence, the familiar frustration

simmering just below the surface. His father spoke as though his entire life had already been written, every step planned and dictated.

'I have plans for you, son,' Ravana continued, his gaze intense. 'Lanka's enemies will fall before you, and you will carry our name across the realms. But you must remain focused. You must remain under control.'

Meghnada's fists clenched. 'Under control?' he echoed, his voice barely concealing the anger that churned within him. 'I am not a child, Father. I have already conquered the heavens. What more do I need to prove?'

Ravana's eyes narrowed. 'You are my heir. You need to prove that you can lead. Power is one thing, but leadership demands more than popularity. The kingdom will not follow someone they do not fear, they need to be ruled with an iron fist.'

'And yet, they follow me!' Meghnada shot back, his voice rising with frustration. 'They love me because I am not you, Father. I do not rule through fear!'

Ravana's face darkened, the simmering rivalry between them finally bubbling to the surface. 'They follow you because they are fools, dazzled by your victories. But the real test will come. When you stand before your enemies, and they challenge not just your strength, but your mind—will you have the control to win?'

'I will not be your shadow forever,' Meghnada retorted, his voice thick with emotion. 'I will carve my path, and it will not be dictated by your fears!'

The silence that followed was heavy, the air between them rife with unspoken tension. Ravana's lips curled into a sneer. 'Do not forget, boy, that everything you have is because of me.'

Meghnada stood, his chest heaving with anger. 'I will not forget, Father. But I will also not be bound by it.'

With that, he stormed from the room, his heart pounding in his chest. Ravana watched him go, his expression unreadable. But deep within, the great king felt a flicker of something he had never expected to feel toward his own son.

Jealousy.

The skies over Lanka darkened, the heavens themselves sensing the growing tension between father and son, one that had long been brewing, now on the verge of eruption. Within the walls of the grand palace, the atmosphere was suffocating, weighed down by the invisible chains that bound them both.

Ravana was a man who had conquered realms, subjugated gods, and ruled Lanka with an iron fist. But here, in the solitude of his thoughts, doubt crept in—a shadow that whispered of his son's growing defiance.

His grip tightened around the armrests of his throne as he replayed their argument in his mind. 'They love me because I am not you.' Meghnada's words echoed in his ears, sharp as a blade. Love. It was a dangerous thing, fleeting and fickle. Ravana had always believed fear was the only true form of control. Fear was constant. Fear made men loyal.

Yet, his people did not fear Meghnada. They admired him. The Thunder Prince, the warrior who commanded storms, who had conquered the heavens. He was everything Ravana had once been—a force of nature, untameable, brimming with ambition. But it was that very ambition that gnawed at Ravana. In Meghnada's rising power, he saw the reflection of his own youth, his own hunger for conquest.

And now, he wondered if he had created a rival instead of an heir.

The door creaked open, and a figure stepped inside—Vibhishana, Ravana's brother. Unlike the mighty king, Vibhishana exuded a quiet, composed strength, his wisdom often contrasting sharply with Ravana's more fiery temperament.

'You seem troubled, brother,' Vibhishana said, his voice calm but probing.

Ravana didn't respond immediately, his gaze fixed on the fire before him. 'It is Meghnada,' he finally said, his voice a low growl. 'He grows restless.'

Vibhishana moved closer, his brow furrowing with concern. 'Restlessness is the curse of youth. It passes with time, as they find their place.'

'He challenges me,' Ravana snapped, turning to face his brother, his eyes burning with frustration. 'He forgets that everything he is, everything he has, comes from me! Yet, he speaks of love, of being his own man, as if I have shackled him.'

'Perhaps he feels... the weight of your expectations,' Vibhishana said carefully. 'You have charted every moment of his life, Ravana. Perhaps he seeks to step out of the shadow cast by your legacy.'

Ravana's lips curled into a sneer. 'I cast no shadow

over him. He is my son. His victories are mine, just as mine are his. There is no difference.'

Vibhishana hesitated, choosing his words with care. 'But perhaps, in his heart, he yearns for something that is his alone. You have trained him to be the perfect warrior, the perfect prince—but not every battle is fought with weapons, Ravana. Perhaps he seeks freedom, not from your power, but from your plans.'

Ravana fell silent, his thoughts churning. The fire crackled, filling the tense pause with its soft hissing. 'I see myself in him,' he admitted, almost begrudgingly. 'That is what troubles me. I see the same hunger, the same need for dominance. But... I also see rebellion.'

'Then perhaps it is time to loosen the chains, brother,' Vibhishana said softly. 'Let him forge his own path, as you once did.'

Ravana scoffed, rising to his feet. 'And let him fall, as I watch from the shadows? No. He will learn as I did—by being forged in fire. He will fight, and he will conquer. But I will be there to guide him.'

Vibhishana nodded, though doubt lingered in his eyes. 'Do not let your pride blind you, Ravana. Meghnada's love for you is not in question. But even the fiercest of sons must one day find his own way.'

As Vibhishana left the room, Ravana stood in silence, the flickering flames casting his expression into shadow. He would not lose his son. Not to defiance, nor to rebellion. But for the first time in his life, Ravana felt something unfamiliar grip his heart.

The fear of being replaced.

The storm had broken over Lanka, and rain lashed the streets with furious intensity. Meghnada stood by the window of his private chambers, watching as lightning cracked across the sky. The storm felt like a mirror to his own inner turmoil—wild, untameable, and filled with an energy he could not control.

His father's words still echoed in his mind. 'You fight as I command.'

Every victory he had won, every conquest, every battle—it had all been dictated by Ravana. Meghnada had grown under his father's watchful eye, moulded into the warrior prince who would one day rule Lanka. But now, with each passing year, the weight of that crown felt heavier. His father's ambitions, his endless thirst for power—Meghnada had inherited them all, but at what cost?

There was no freedom in being Ravana's heir. No space for his own dreams, his own desires. And that, more than anything, had begun to suffocate him.

His thoughts turned to Sulochana. She had been the one bright spot in his life, a decision that had been entirely his own. Their marriage had been an act of defiance, a break from the iron grip of his father's control. Sulochana saw him not as the prince, not as Ravana's son, but as Meghnada—the man beneath the crown.

The door to his chamber creaked open, and she stepped inside, her presence like a calming breeze in the storm. 'You've been quiet since your return,' she said softly, approaching him. 'What troubles you?'

Meghnada turned to her, his face etched with frustration. 'It is my father,' he admitted, his voice heavy with emotion. 'He does not see me. He only sees the legacy he has created, the image of himself that he has shaped me into.'

Sulochana placed a hand on his arm, her touch gentle, grounding. 'You are more than that, Meghnada. You have already proven yourself, to the heavens and to the people of Lanka. They love you for who you are, not for who your father wants you to be.'

'But I am still in his shadow,' Meghnada said, his voice thick with the weight of years spent trying to measure up. 'Everything I do, everything I achieve, is his victory, not mine. I want to be more than just his son. I want to be something... different.'

Sulochana studied him for a moment, her eyes filled with understanding. 'Then you must take that step, Meghnada. No one else can do it for you. You must decide what kind of man you wish to be, and you must make that choice with conviction.'

Meghnada closed his eyes for a moment, letting her words sink in. She was right. He had always fought for his father, for his name, for Lanka. But now, he had to fight for himself.

'I will,' he said, his voice resolute. 'But I will not defy him openly. I will find my own path, but it will be one that brings honour to my name—and to his.'

Sulochana smiled, though there was a hint of sadness in her eyes. 'I know you will. But know this, Meghnada—your father's shadow is long, and it will not be easy to escape.'

'I don't want to escape it,' Meghnada replied, his voice hardening. 'I want to outshine it.'

In the days that followed, the tension between father and son only grew. Ravana, though proud of Meghnada's victories, began to see the subtle changes in his son's demeanour. Meghnada's outbursts, once rare, became more frequent, his frustration with the constraints of his role bubbling to the surface. The court whispered of the growing divide between the two, though none dared to speak openly about it.

The Rakshasas loved Meghnada, and that love only deepened Ravana's sense of rivalry. He could feel the power slipping through his fingers, even as he tried to tighten his grip. Meghnada was no longer just his heir—he was becoming a force in his own right, a symbol of change that Ravana could not entirely comprehend or control.

One evening, after a particularly heated exchange with his father, Meghnada retreated to the rooftops of the palace. The wind whipped through his hair, and the distant sounds of the city reached his ears—a reminder of the world that lay beyond the walls of the palace.

He stood there, looking out over the city he would one day rule, his thoughts churning like the storm clouds above. He loved his father, that much was true. But he could no longer live in the shadow of a man who saw him as nothing more than an extension of his own power.

Power, he thought bitterly, the word tasting like ash on his tongue. It was all his father ever spoke of. But what was power without freedom? Without purpose?

As the rain began to fall, Meghnada made a decision. He would no longer be bound by the chains of his father's ambitions. He would fight for Lanka, for his people—but he would do it on his own terms.

And in that moment, standing beneath the stormy sky, Meghnada felt something he had not felt in years.

Freedom.

TWENTY

The Abduction of Sita

Lustful Revenge

Akampana, Ravana's uncle and a trusted general, rushed into the throne room of Lanka, visibly shaken and out of breath. Without any formalities, he blurted out the grim news, 'Maharaja Ravana, all the Rakshasas of Janasthana have been slain. Khara and Dushana are no more, and your sister Minakshi has been mutilated!'

Ravana was shocked, and immediately furious afterwards. His face darkened as he leapt up from his throne. His booming voice reverberated through the hall, 'What is it that you speak of, Akampana? Who has dared to destroy such a formidable army? What happened to Minakshi? Tell me who killed Khara and Dushana. I will not rest until I exterminate them!'

Akampana, though shaken, gathered himself and recounted the events that had transpired in Janasthana. Minakshi had come running into their Rakshasa dwelling in the forest, disfigured and humiliated. Her ears and nose had been cut off. Blood poured down her face as she cried out for her cousins, 'Khara! Dushana! Help me!'

Khara and Dushana, enraged by the sight of their

cousin's mutilation, immediately assembled their army of forest Rakshasas and led a fierce charge against the two men responsible—Rama and Lakshmana—apparently the exiled sons of King Dasharatha of Ayodhya. However, despite their might and numbers, the Rakshasas were no match for the princes. Akampana, the lone survivor of that massacre, had fled the battlefield in terror and came directly to Ravana to deliver the news.

'Rama and Lakshmana cut down our entire army with ease. Both Khara and Dushana have perished in the battle,' Akampana wailed, 'the forest is littered with the bodies of Rakshasa warriors, their blood staining the earth.'

As he recounted Rama's incredible feats in battle, Akampana could not hide the fear and awe he felt. But Ravana, known for his arrogance and pride in his own unmatched strength, dismissed the danger. His voice was filled with bravado, 'I will kill this miserable human without delay.'

Akampana, however, knew better. 'Maharaja,' he said, choosing his words carefully, 'I beg of you to listen. Defeating Rama is not as simple as you think. He is no ordinary human. His prowess is extraordinary, and with his brother Lakshmana by his side, they form a formidable duo. Even the strongest forces would struggle to defeat them. Sending another army against them will only lead to more deaths. I have a plan, and I urge you to consider it.'

Ravana nodded slowly and sat down. The Rakshasas were dead, and there was no need for an immediate and impulsive reaction. He leaned forward. 'What is your plan, Akampana? Speak.'

Akampana explained, 'Maharaja, Rama is accompanied by a young woman—his wife, Sita. She is unparalleled in beauty. I have never seen a woman as lovely as her, be it among gods or mortals. Rama is deeply devoted to her. If you can somehow abduct her, Rama will be consumed by grief. He will forget everything—his strength, his duty, even food and drink. In his despair, he will waste away and die. And you, Maharaja, will possess this beautiful woman.'

Ravana pondered this suggestion. The plan seemed good, and the idea of punishing this man Rama while acquiring a woman of beauty appealed to his ego. Thus, Ravana summoned his chariot and set out on a journey to seek the counsel of his sorcerer uncle, Maricha.

When he reached Maricha's dwelling, Ravana wasted no time in recounting the events—the death of Khara and Dushana and the annihilation of his army at the hands of Rama. He then revealed his plan for vengeance: he would abduct Sita, Rama's beloved wife, and for this, he needed Maricha's help.

'You will take the form of a golden deer,' Ravana explained, 'and lure Rama away from his wife. Once he is gone, I will seize her and bring her back to Lanka.'

Maricha transformed into a golden deer, and Ravana's cunning plan was set into motion. Ravana's eyes gleamed as he watched the glittering creature move through the forest, knowing it would lure Rama away from Sita. Maricha had obeyed Ravana's commands reluctantly, but the transformation was flawless—an exquisite creature that gleamed in the sun, mesmerising anyone who beheld it. Even from a distance, the creature was a sight to behold, its golden pelt shimmering like the finest jewels.

It wasn't long before Sita's gaze fell upon the deer, and she was immediately entranced. 'Rama! Look at that beautiful deer!' she exclaimed, her voice filled with childlike wonder. Her eyes sparkled with delight as she tugged on Rama's arm. 'Please, catch it and bring it to me! I must have it!'

Rama frowned, sensing something unnatural. Lakshmana was just as suspicious. 'Golden deer don't exist,' he said sharply, his instincts flaring. 'This is clearly a trick. Stay here, brother. Do not chase after this illusion.' But Sita, her heart set on possessing the creature, would not be swayed. She pleaded with Rama, her eyes wide with longing. 'Please, my lord, catch it for me.'

Rama hesitated only for a moment before his love for Sita overcame his doubts. 'Lakshmana, stay here and protect her,' he ordered, his tone serious. 'I'll go after the deer.' With that, Rama dashed into the forest, following the elusive creature deeper and deeper into the trees, unaware that he was falling into Ravana's carefully laid trap.

For a time, everything was silent, the peaceful hum of the forest settling around their hut. But soon, the air was filled with the distant sound of Rama's voice, shouting for help. Sita's heart leapt in her chest, fear clawing at her as she turned to Lakshmana. 'He is in trouble!' she cried, her voice thick with panic. 'Go help him!'

Lakshmana stood his ground, his eyes steely. 'No, devi. My brother is invincible. This is not what it seems—it's a trick, I'm certain of it. He told me to stay here, and I must follow his orders.'

But Sita, blinded by worry and desperation, was not so easily convinced. 'You care nothing for him!' she spat, her voice sharp with accusation. 'You stand here while my husband is in mortal danger. What kind of brother are you?'

Lakshmana winced at her words, the accusation cutting deeper than any blade. Reluctantly, he relented, but not before drawing his sword and tracing a line in the earth around the hut. His face was grave as he turned to Sita. 'I am going, but heed my words. Do not cross this line under any circumstances. It will protect you from harm until I return with my brother.'

With that, Lakshmana left, his form disappearing into the trees as Sita stood alone. She paced anxiously, glancing in the direction both brothers had gone, her heart heavy with dread. Time seemed to stretch, each second dragging like an eternity.

A figure emerged from the trees—a humble ascetic, clad in saffron robes, a begging bowl in hand. His voice was soft, almost pleading. 'Mother,' he called, bowing slightly. 'I have come for alms. May you not refuse a poor wanderer?'

Sita's heart softened at the sight of the old man. But she hesitated, remembering Lakshmana's warning. The line in the dirt shimmered faintly under the sunlight, a silent reminder of the protection it offered. 'Please, come closer, holy one,' she said, keeping her distance.

'I will gladly give you what you need.'

But the ascetic shook his head, his voice growing stern. 'I cannot cross the threshold of your home uninvited, mother. Come closer and place the alms in my bowl, for it is your dharma to serve those in need.'

Torn between her duty and Lakshmana's warning, Sita's hand trembled. Surely, a holy man could not mean her harm, she thought. Driven by a sense of righteousness and obligation, Sita took a step forward and crossed the *Lakshmana Rekha.*

The moment her foot crossed the line, the ascetic's form began to shift and twist, and in his place stood the towering figure of Ravana, the King of Lanka. His laughter boomed through the clearing, deep and terrible, as his twenty arms reached out to seize her. 'Foolish woman,' he growled, his voice dripping with malice. 'You are mine now!'

Sita screamed and struggled in Ravana's ironclad grip. He dragged her toward the *Pushpaka Vimana,* a chariot as black as night, its wheels turning with the speed of the wind.

Sita's terrified cries of protest echoed through the forest. Ravana revelled in his triumph, savouring his moment of victory over the woman whose abduction would bring her husband to his knees.

The *Pushpaka Vimana,* lifted off the ground with the force of the wind, hurtling toward Lanka. Ravana laughed cruelly, his twenty arms bristling with power as he held Sita. 'Rama will never find you, my dear. You've vanished without a trace!' He could almost taste the sweetness of his revenge, imagining Rama's anguish as he discovered his beloved wife had been taken.

But as Ravana flew higher into the sky, a shadow loomed over him. A deafening cry pierced the air, and suddenly the mighty eagle Jatayu appeared. His massive wings cut through the sky as he dove toward the chariot, his sharp talons aimed at Ravana's head. Jatayu had seen Ravana's vile act and was determined to stop him, even at the cost of his own life.

'Release her, Ravana!' Jatayu roared, his voice thunderous and filled with righteous fury. The eagle's beak and claws were relentless as he slashed at Ravana's body, drawing blood. Sita, her heart pounding with hope, watched the battle unfold, praying desperately for Jatayu's victory.

Ravana, caught off guard by the sudden attack, grunted in pain as Jatayu's talons dug into his flesh. But his arrogance knew no bounds. 'Foolish bird! You dare challenge the might of Ravana?' he bellowed, unsheathing his sword. The two clashed mid-air, the sound of metal against talon ringing through the skies.

Jatayu swooped and dived, pecking and clawing at Ravana with all his might. His feathers bristled with determination, but Ravana was no easy opponent. The Rakshasa king swung his sword with brutal precision, aiming to sever Jatayu's wings. Blood sprayed from Ravana's wounds as Jatayu tore into him, yet the eagle's blows were not enough to slow him down.

Despite his age, Jatayu fought valiantly, his powerful wings propelling him toward Ravana again and again.

But with each clash, Ravana grew more enraged. His sword flashed in the sunlight, and in a moment of vicious strength, he sliced into Jatayu's wing. The eagle screeched in agony, but still, he fought on, refusing to let Ravana escape with Sita.

'You are no match for me, Jatayu!' Ravana shouted, his voice booming with rage. 'I am the lord of all Rakshasas. You will die for your insolence!'

With a final, devastating blow, Ravana's sword severed Jatayu's wings completely. The once-mighty bird, now crippled and drenched in blood, spiralled toward the earth. As he fell, his eyes locked with Sita's, filled with sorrow and an unspoken apology. Ravana watched with cold satisfaction as Jatayu plummeted to the ground, a broken and defeated warrior.

Sita screamed, tears streaming down her face as she watched her protector fall. Jatayu had fought bravely, but even his strength was no match for the merciless might of Ravana. 'May your corpse rot in this forsaken forest!' Ravana snarled as he urged the *Pushpaka Vimana* onward.

Turning his gaze toward Sita, Ravana's eyes glittered with dark triumph. 'No one can save you now,' he said, his voice dripping with malice. 'Not your husband, not that foolish bird. You belong to me, and once we reach Lanka, you will understand the futility of resisting my will.'

Ravana's *Pushpaka Vimana* descended upon Lanka, its golden spires gleaming in the sunlight, over the deep azure waters of the ocean below. Ravana wasted no time as he stepped out with Sita in tow, his gaze filled with desire and the thrills of conquest as he led her toward his towering palace. The grandeur of Lanka seemed to pulse with his triumph, yet Sita remained unmoved, her eyes distant as she thought only of Rama.

As they climbed the palace steps, Mandodari rushed to Ravana, her face pale with concern. 'My lord,' she implored, her voice trembling slightly, 'don't bring this woman into our home. She does not belong here. You bring disaster to our house by having abducted her against her will. She will bring ruin upon us!'

Ravana stopped in his tracks. Mandodari's words had pierced through his moment of pride and triggered a long-forgotten memory. For an instant, a shadow crossed his mind. He remembered Nalakuvara, the son of Kubera, whom he had once wronged. Nalakuvara had cursed Ravana that his head would explode into a thousand pieces if he ever forced himself upon a woman without her consent. There were some limits that even he, the great Ravana, with his nearly limitless powers, could not transgress.

Suppressing his frustration, Ravana turned to his servants. 'Take this woman to the Ashoka Vatika,' he commanded, his voice cold. 'She will remain there until she comes to her senses.'

Sita was taken to the beautiful but isolated garden, far from the palace's main chambers. Ravana's voice followed her, his tone low and menacing. 'I will wait, Sita. Sooner or later, you will change your mind and accept me.'

With that, Ravana turned to go up the palace stairs, leaving Sita alone in her sorrow, as Rakshasi guards closed in around her.

TWENTY-ONE

Lanka on Fire

The Knell of War

News of Vali's death came to Ravana through his skilled network of spies, men trained to collect and deliver vital intelligence from even the most distant lands. One morning, as Ravana sat in his grand court, a messenger from his spy network approached, his face grim. Ravana, sensing the gravity of the situation, motioned for him to speak.

'Maharaja,' the spy began, his voice low but clear, 'King Vali of Kishkindha is dead.'

Ravana's eyes flashed with surprise and sudden rage. Vali, the invincible Vanara king, known for his unparalleled strength and prowess, was no easy prey. 'Who dares kill Vali?' Ravana demanded, his tone laden with disbelief. The spy reported that Vali had fallen in combat, not to an army or a warrior of equal strength, but to a single arrow fired in stealth by a prince named Rama, who had allied with Vali's estranged brother, Sugriva.

Ravana's fingers clenched the armrest of his throne. Vali had been a friend, a mighty ally whom he respected for his strength and loyalty. To learn that he was felled by deception enraged the king of Lanka. 'An arrow from the shadows?' Ravana muttered. 'Cowardice!'

Although the spy did not know much about Rama, Ravana's keen mind began to make the connections. This was the same Rama whose wife, Sita, now resided in his custody. His intelligence had earlier indicated Rama's presence in the forest, but the connection to Vali's death sharpened the threat. He now began to realise that this Rama was no ordinary man; he was a dangerous adversary.

Several months had passed when one day, reports of a monkey wreaking havoc reached Ravana's court.

The messenger's breathless report stoked Ravana's fury further. 'The Vanara is called Hanuman. He has reduced the Ashoka Vatika to a wasteland,' the guard stammered. 'Trees are uprooted, the guards have been thrown aside like bundles of straw, and he has caused great panic within the palace grounds.'

Ravana's face twisted in fury. The Ashoka Vatika, his personal sanctuary, where he kept Sita imprisoned, had been desecrated by a mere monkey. He could not allow such an affront to go unpunished.

He sent his young son, Akshay, a valiant and formidable warrior, to subdue the rampaging creature. Akshay sped towards the Ashoka Vatika, eager to prove himself. As he approached, he saw the Vanara standing amidst the destruction.

With a furious war cry, Akshay unleashed his attacks. Arrows flew from his bow, and his chariot charged forward like a storm. But Hanuman, with the agility he had by virtue of being the wind god's son, leapt into the air, dodging the arrows effortlessly. The young prince was undeterred and pressed forward with his attacks, but nothing seemed to work. Hanuman's immense strength and divine prowess were beyond anything Akshay had faced before.

Then, with one powerful leap, Hanuman landed atop Akshay's chariot, shattering it beneath his feet. The Rakshasa prince barely had time to react before Hanuman grabbed him by the legs and swung him violently through the air, dashing him against the ground. The impact was fatal and Akshay's body lay lifeless.

When the news of Akshay's death reached Ravana, the demon king was shattered. How could this be? How could a creature so lowly dare to challenge his might and kill one of his sons?

With a slow, deliberate voice, Ravana turned to his most powerful son, Meghnada, known across the three worlds as Indrajit—the conqueror of Indra. 'Go,' he commanded, his voice trembling. 'Bring this beast before me. But do not kill him just yet—I wish to see him suffer.'

Hanuman continued to unleash chaos across Lanka, knowing full well that he would soon face greater forces. But he welcomed the confrontation. He had a message to deliver, and he would stop at nothing to ensure that it reached the ears of the demon king.

Meghnada swiftly departed, and within hours, the court received word that the monkey had been captured. Soon after, the monkey was dragged into Ravana's court in chains. Ravana, eager to assess this strange being for himself, fixed his gaze on the bound creature. The Vanara's eyes burned with defiance despite his restraints, and Ravana could see that this was no ordinary emissary.

As Hanuman stood before the demon king, something extraordinary occurred. Hanuman began to stretch his tail—lengthening it, winding it upward in spirals until he could sit on it like a throne. Ravana's ministers gasped in astonishment as they realised that Hanuman was now sitting higher than Ravana himself. It was a gesture of deliberate defiance, an affront to the king's supremacy.

Furious, Ravana ordered his strongest warriors to seize the monkey and push him to the ground. But when they tried to lift Hanuman's tail, not a single Rakshasa, no matter how mighty, could budge it. Even Ravana, despite his great strength, failed to lift the tail. Ravana's anger grew with each failed attempt.

Calmly, Hanuman spoke at last. 'I am the emissary of Rama, prince of Ayodhya. I have come to warn you, Ravana. Return Sita to her rightful husband, or face the destruction of Lanka. My lord will come for her, and when he does, you will be powerless to stop him.'

Ravana, seething with fury, dismissed Hanuman's words as empty threats. 'Burn his tail,' he roared. 'Let the flames be a lesson to him and his kind about defying the king of Lanka.'

The Rakshasas immediately soaked Hanuman's tail in oil and set it ablaze. But as soon as the flames erupted from his tail, Hanuman, with a roar of defiance, broke free from his bonds. Using his now fiery tail as a weapon, he began leaping across the city, setting buildings, palaces, and homes alight with every strike.

Lanka, the golden city, was soon engulfed in flames. Ravana's subjects screamed in terror as the fire spread through the streets, the flames consuming the wealth and grandeur of the demon king's kingdom. Hanuman had become a one-Vanara army, turning Ravana's arrogance into ashes.

Amid the chaos, Hanuman leapt to the skies, his mission complete. He had delivered Rama's message, surveyed the enemy's strength, and left a burning reminder of Rama's power. With one final bound, Hanuman crossed the ocean and escaped back to the safety of his people, leaving Ravana to face the smouldering ruins of his once-mighty city.

In his palace, Ravana stood in silence, watching the black smoke spiralling into the sky. His rage was now laced with a sense of impending doom. The Vanara's words echoed in his mind. He knew the fight for Sita had only just begun.

Soon, Ravana received word that a massive army of Vanaras, led by Rama, had gathered on the mainland coasts across the sea. This report would have unnerved any other ruler, but Ravana's lips curled into a mocking smile. 'A horde of monkeys dare to threaten me, the great Ravana?' His deep voice echoed across the vast chamber. 'Lanka's golden walls have never been breached, and they will never fall to mere beasts!'

His ministers and courtiers agreed with murmurs

of assent, their faces eager to mirror the confidence of their king. Yet, one figure remained silent—Vibhishana, Ravana's younger brother. As the others revelled in their apparent invulnerability, Vibhishana's heart was heavy. He had sensed the growing menace in Rama's approach, and he knew that dismissing the threat would be a grievous mistake.

Requesting that he be heard, Vibhishana spoke, his voice steady but firm. 'Brother, these Vanaras you scorn indeed appear to be disorganised. But do not be deceived by their form. They are led by Rama, who is no ordinary man. He and his Vanara army will not be stopped by the fortifications of Lanka.'

Ravana's brows furrowed, and his expression darkened. He stood from his throne, towering over his younger brother. 'Vibhishana, you speak as if you admire this human! Have you forgotten who I am? Have you forgotten the powers that I possess?'

The tension in the room thickened as Vibhishana bravely continued, 'Brother, I speak out of concern for Lanka and for you. If you return Sita to Rama and make peace, perhaps our kingdom can be spared from the devastation that looms.'

A voice from the back of the chamber interrupted Vibhishana's plea. It was Meghnada. The prince stepped forward, a gleam of battle-lust in his eyes. 'Uncle, how dare you insult the might of Lanka by suggesting we yield to these forest-dwellers? I, Meghnada, have defeated the king of gods in battle. I shall crush this Rama and his monkey horde before they even set foot on our sacred soil.'

The court erupted in applause at Meghnada's fiery words, but Vibhishana remained undeterred. 'Bravery and arrogance are not the same, Meghnada,' he said calmly. 'Do not underestimate Rama.'

Ravana could no longer contain his rage. 'Enough!' he thundered, his voice booming through the hall. 'I will not have your cowardly lectures in my court, Vibhishana! If you are so enamoured by this human, perhaps you should leave Lanka and join him!'

Vibhishana, his heart heavy with sorrow, realised that there was no more he could do to sway his brother from his path of destruction. 'You have lost your way, Ravana,' he said, his voice filled with regret. 'But I will not lose mine.' With those words, Vibhishana turned and left the royal court.

The courtiers watched in stunned silence. Ravana stood still, his hands clenched into fists, seething with fury at the betrayal. But within his heart, a flicker of doubt began to stir—though his pride would never let him admit it.

Vibhishana immediately made his way to the shores across the sea, and arrived at the camp of Rama and his army. He joined their cause, pledging his loyalty to Rama, even as Ravana prepared for the battle that would decide the fate of Lanka.

The tension in the Lankan court was palpable as Ravana received alarming news from his spies. The mighty Sea Lord Varuna had helped Rama and his massive Vanara army by allowing the construction of a bridge across the sea—a feat accomplished in just five days. What had once seemed impossible was now a reality. An invading army stood at the coasts of Lanka, their war cries echoing as they marched across the newly built bridge.

Ravana, sitting in his throne room, felt beads of sweat forming on his forehead as his informants described the scene of hordes of Vanaras swarming towards the shores of his once impenetrable island. Yet, he scoffed, his pride and confidence unshaken. 'Let them come,' he shouted angrily, certain of his impregnable fortress and his indomitable power.

His ministers exchanged nervous glances. The scale of the enemy army could not be ignored, and Varuna's involvement had an ominous significance. Ravana's apparent confidence masked a deeper fear that he would never admit aloud.

Outside the city, Rama and his Vanara army set up camp just beyond the ramparts of Lanka. The prince of Ayodhya decided to send one last message to the king of Lanka. Angada, the brave son of Vali, was dispatched to Ravana's court as an emissary of peace.

Angada arrived at Ravana's grand hall, his eyes gleaming with resolve. The Rakshasa king eyed him with disdain, but there was a flicker of recognition; Vali had been Ravana's friend, and here stood his son, now an enemy.

'I come with a message from Rama,' Angada began, his voice echoing through the halls. 'He offers you one final chance to avoid this war. Return Sita, to her rightful place by his side. Spare your kingdom the destruction that awaits if you persist in your defiance.'

Ravana's face contorted in anger. 'Your father, Vali, was a great friend of mine! You dare stand before me with such demands?!' His voice dripped with arrogance and fury. 'Tell your leader, I do not fear his army, nor his threats. Sita is mine, and I will not bow to a mere human.'

Angada remained calm. 'The days of your reign are numbered, Ravana. This is not a threat—it is a promise. If you refuse, Lanka will be overrun.'

The two locked eyes, their verbal sparring growing more intense. Ravana hurled insults at Rama and the Vanaras, but Angada was unmoved. Finally, Angada issued a challenge. 'Before you decide to face the wrath of our army, I challenge you to move my foot.'

Ravana's courtiers, insulted by the audacity of the young Vanara, rushed forward. They strained and struggled, pulling at Angada's foot with all their might, but it did not budge, not even by a fraction. Ravana, furious, rose from his throne and approached. Bending down to take hold of Angada's foot, the Vanara prince leaned in and whispered, 'Would it not be better to clasp the feet of Rama, rather than waste your strength here?'

At that moment, Ravana's crown, his pride and his power, slipped and fell to the ground. Humiliated, Ravana returned to his seat in silence. Angada, in one swift motion, scooped it up and flung it in the direction of the Rakshasa King.

'This was your last chance, Ravana. Prepare for your funeral.'

The hall fell into a shocked silence watching their king's abject insult inside his own court. Without another word, Angada turned on his heel and left the court, his final challenge hanging in the air. No one dared to stop him.

Ravana, seething with fury, sat back on his throne, the humiliation cutting deeper than any wound. War was inevitable, and now it was personal.

TWENTY-TWO

A Titan Falls

The Loyal Giant

The war between Rama's Vanara army and Ravana's Rakshasas would go on for eighty-seven days.

The war drums echoed across the battlefield, rolling like thunder through the dense clouds of ash and dust. The vast Vanara army, led by Sugriva, Rama, and Lakshmana, stretched as far as the eye could see. The mighty Vanaras were armed with stones, uprooted trees, and their own brute strength. Hanuman, his mighty form gleaming like bronze, moved among the soldiers, a tower of resolve. Beside him stood Nila and Angada, ready to lead the first assault. Lakshmana's face was a mask of quiet determination, his bow strung tight at his side.

Behind the towering walls, smoke billowed from iron towers, the air thick with the smell of coal and fire.

Across the battleground, Ravana sat high in his throne, gazing out from the iron parapets of Lanka. His eyes burned with fury, though his face remained still. His generals, dark Rakshasas clad in black iron, murmured nervously among themselves. Ravana's fingers drummed against the arm of his throne. His spies had returned with reports of Rama's approach, but he had known this day would come long before they confirmed it.

'They think they can breach my gates?' Ravana's voice was a deep rumble. He looked to his generals. 'Let them try.'

He raised his hand, and at his command, the gates of Lanka groaned open. Out poured legions of Rakshasas, monstrous beings with weapons forged in the fires of Lanka. They roared and howled as they marched forward, the ground trembling under their weight.

'Today, Ravana, we claim victory!' Nila shouted, his voice rising above the thunderous march. He raised a great tree trunk above his head and hurled it toward the advancing Rakshasa ranks.

The tree crashed down with the force of a mountain, scattering Rakshasas like leaves in a storm. The battle erupted in full, with Vanaras leaping over the walls, tearing at the fortifications with bare hands and sharp stones. Ravana's forces retaliated fiercely, their dark arrows cutting through the sky like a swarm of black birds. Screams echoed across the battlefield as the first blood was spilled, Vanaras and Rakshasas locked in mortal combat.

From the distance, Rama and Lakshmana observed, their faces grim. Rama's hand rested on the *Kodanda*, his legendary bow. He spoke softly, almost to himself. 'This is just the beginning.'

Above them, the sky was a pale gold, the dawn of battle's first day.

A day ago, Ravana had sent out his spies to gather intelligence on the strength of Rama's forces. Upon hearing the reports, he realised the time for subterfuge had passed. He ordered his army to prepare for battle, fortifying the walls of his city and sending his generals to the front lines.

Almost immediately, the Vanaras attacked the gates of Lanka. Rama's trusted generals—Nila, Nala, Hanuman, and Angada—led the assault. Stones, trees, and raw strength were the weapons of the Vanara army, while the Rakshasas met them with arrows, spears, and dark sorcery. Throughout the day, skirmishes raged along the walls, but neither side gained a decisive advantage.

Both Rama and Ravana watched the battle unfold, holding back their full strength for the right moment.

By dawn of the second day, the battlefield was drenched in blood, the air heavy with the stench of death. Ravana, sitting in the heart of Lanka, could feel the tension building, his patience wearing thin. His generals were losing ground. The Vanaras were relentless.

Ravana stood, his tall frame casting a long shadow over the Rakshasa lords. 'Enough,' he muttered, gripping his bow with hands like iron. His eyes narrowed, gleaming like molten gold. 'I will crush them myself.'

He descended from his throne, donning his dark armour. Every piece of it was forged from the blackest iron, its edges sharp and cold. As he mounted his chariot, drawn by black horses with fiery eyes, his presence filled the battlefield with an unnatural cold. The earth trembled at his approach.

'Rama!' Ravana roared, his voice thundering across the battlefield. His chariot raced forward, his bow singing as he let loose arrows that seemed to tear through the very fabric of the sky. The arrows shrieked through the air, each one striking true, cutting down Vanaras with deadly precision. Blood spattered across the battlefield, soaking the earth in crimson.

Rama, seeing the devastation, stepped forward. He raised his own bow, the *Kodanda*, its string thrumming with power as he drew it back. His eyes were locked on Ravana.

'Your terror ends today, Ravana!' Rama's voice was calm but filled with steely resolve.

Their arrows clashed in the air, shattering in blinding bursts of light and sound. Ravana's face twisted into a snarl as he unleashed more arrows, faster and fiercer, each one laced with dark magic. They shrieked like banshees as they tore toward Rama, but he met them with equal force, his arrows glowing with divine energy.

'You are strong, Rama, but strength alone will not save you from me!' Ravana growled, vanishing from sight in a burst of dark energy. He reappeared behind Rama, his sword raised high, ready to strike.

But Rama was swift. He spun and blocked the blow with the shaft of his bow, the force of the impact sending a shockwave through the battlefield. Sparks flew as their weapons clashed again and again, the sound of steel on steel echoing across the field.

Lakshmana, sensing his brother's danger, rushed to his side. 'Brother!' he shouted, his sword drawn.

Rama held up a hand, his eyes never leaving Ravana. 'This fight is mine, Lakshmana.'

The two warriors clashed until dusk, neither giving

an inch. But as the shadows lengthened, Ravana, growing frustrated, disappeared once again, retreating to the safety of his city.

The battlefield fell quiet after their first clash. Days turned into weeks as both armies took time to regroup. The Vanaras celebrated their small victory, bolstering morale while the injured were tended to by the best healers. Meanwhile, Ravana plotted his revenge, gathering his forces and fortifying his defences.

A council of his commanders met in the grand hall of Lanka, the tension palpable. 'We cannot underestimate Rama,' Ravana warned, his voice a low growl. 'He is stronger than we anticipated. We will strike again, and this time, I will not hold back.'

Once the new moon rose, the battle resumed. The battlefield shook under a blood-red sky when Ravana sent one of his most powerful generals, Prahastha, to lead the Rakshasa forces. Mounted on his chariot, Prahastha stormed the battlefield, wreaking havoc among the Vanara ranks. His dark magic and brutal strength seemed unstoppable, and the morale among Rama's army wavered.

Rama sent Nila, one of his foremost commanders, to confront the Rakshasa general. Their duel was fierce, and Prahastha's strength began to overpower Nila. Just as Prahastha prepared to deliver a fatal blow, Hanuman intervened, using his great strength to hold the demon back. Together, Nila and Hanuman fought Prahasta until Nila, with one final mighty strike, brought the demon general to his knees, killing him.

The death of Prahastha dealt a significant blow to Ravana's army. One by one, Mahaparshva, Virupaksha and many other Rakshasa generals fell. Demoralised, the Rakshasas retreated behind the walls of Lanka once more.

Enraged by their failure, Ravana called upon his brother, Kumbhakarna, who slumbered deep within the bowels of the city.

'Kumbhakarna!' Ravana's voice echoed through the cavernous halls. The giant stirred, his enormous body shifting as he slowly awoke from his cursed slumber. His eyes opened, glowing like molten lava.

'What is it, brother?' Kumbhakarna's voice rumbled like an earthquake.

'I need you,' Ravana said, his voice cold. 'The battle turns against us. Only you can crush these wretched beings.'

Kumbhakarna rose, his massive form towering over even the tallest Rakshasas. His footsteps shook the ground as he strode onto the battlefield. The Vanaras froze at the sight of him, their courage faltering.

He waded into the Vanara ranks, his hands crushing and tearing, his feet stomping down like boulders. The Vanaras attacked with all their might, but no weapon seemed to harm him. Trees shattered against his skin, stones bounced harmlessly off his chest.

Rama, seeing the carnage, stepped forward, his bow

drawn. The two titans clashed, Rama's arrows striking Kumbhakarna with the force of a storm. For hours they fought, and though Kumbhakarna's strength seemed limitless, Rama's precision slowly wore him down. Each arrow struck a vital point, weakening the giant.

Finally, with a divine arrow, Rama severed Kumbhakarna's head. The massive body staggered, then fell, crashing to the earth with a sound like mountains breaking. The ground trembled as Kumbhakarna's lifeless form lay still.

TWENTY-THREE

The Thunder of the Clouds

Master of Illusions

With his brother dead, Ravana's heart darkened with rage. But he was not yet defeated. He called upon his son, Meghnada, or Indrajit, the master of sorcery.

'Go, my son,' Ravana commanded, his voice low and dangerous. 'Show them the true power of Lanka.'

Meghnada nodded, his eyes gleaming with dark magic. He mounted his chariot and rode into battle. His horses, snorting with fury, dragged his chariot across the blood-soaked earth as Meghnada reached the front lines.

Rama's army watched as the Rakshasa prince arrived, and Lakshmana, standing tall beside his brother, felt the unmistakable pull of battle growing closer. Meghnada, armoured in dark steel and wrapped in an aura of malevolent power, raised his hand to halt his advancing forces.

'I am Indrajit!' he bellowed, his voice echoing across the field. 'He who has vanquished even the gods shall show you the price of defying Lanka! Who among you dares face me?'

Without hesitation, Lakshmana stepped forward, gripping his bow with an unyielding resolve. His gaze was unwavering as he met Meghnada's challenge. 'I will face you, Indrajit,' Lakshmana said, his voice calm but edged with defiance. 'Your sorcery will not shield you from justice.'

Meghnada's eyes narrowed, and he smiled, a cruel smile full of arrogance and confidence. 'You think you can match me, prince of Ayodhya? Very well, let us see if your bravery lasts when you face the wrath of the son of Ravana.'

Lakshmana's face remained focused as he drew back his bowstring again, firing arrow after arrow, each one aimed with deadly precision. But Meghnada was no ordinary foe. With every volley of Lakshmana's divine arrows, the Rakshasa prince countered with bolts of his own magic, deflecting them with ease.

'I am no mortal to be felled by mere arrows!' Meghnada shouted as he conjured a massive spear of pure energy and hurled it toward Lakshmana. Lakshmana barely had time to dodge, the spear brushing past his armour and slamming into the ground behind him, leaving a smoking crater where it struck.

Undeterred, Lakshmana retaliated with an arrow that blazed like fire, striking Meghnada's chariot with such force that the entire vehicle shuddered. Meghnada let out a roar of rage.

'This is where it ends for you, Lakshmana,' Meghnada growled. 'You shall fall, and with you, the hopes of Rama.' With a flick of his hand, Meghnada cast a powerful illusion, vanishing from sight. His chariot, his figure, his very presence dissolved into the swirling darkness, leaving no trace. The battlefield fell eerily silent as Rama's army looked around in confusion, their enemy now invisible to all.

Lakshmana gripped his bow tighter, his eyes scanning the skies and the ground. He knew Meghnada had not retreated, but hidden himself within a veil of sorcery. 'Do not be fooled by his tricks!' Lakshmana called to the Vanaras. 'Stay vigilant!'

But even as he spoke, the first strike of Meghnada's illusion came without warning. Ghostly arrows seemed to materialise out of thin air, raining down upon the Vanara army with deadly precision. Lakshmana raised his shield, deflecting the onslaught, but the Vanaras were caught off guard, many falling to the unseen assault. Chaos erupted as the soldiers tried to regroup, the enemy now a phantom in the air.

Meghnada, hidden from view, laughed cruelly as he unleashed bolt after bolt of magical energy, his attacks coming from every direction at once. 'This is the power of sorcery, Lakshmana! You cannot defeat what you cannot see!'

The Rakshasa prince unleashed his most powerful weapon—the *Nagapasha*[*], a magical serpent-arrow that

---

*Indrajit uses the Nagapasha (serpent-noose) and succeeds in binding only Lakshmana, leaving Rama free.

That incident is not in Valmiki's text (there both brothers are bound together), but it does occur in a handful of later, still-authoritative Sanskrit and vernacular recensions.

The clearest, most widely cited account is in Adhyatma-Ramayana, Yuddha-kanda 9.15–9.46.

coiled through the air with deadly purpose. The serpent hissed as it flew, its eyes gleaming like burning embers, seeking Lakshmana's heart.

Before anyone could react, the arrow struck, and the serpent's coils wrapped themselves tightly around Lakshmana. He gasped in agony as the magical bonds constricted, squeezing the life from his body. The Rakshasa magic was potent, draining his strength with every breath. Lakshmana's knees buckled, and he fell to the ground, his body limp, his face pale as death.

'Brother!' Rama's voice tore through the chaos as he rushed to Lakshmana's side, cradling his brother's body in his arms. His heart ached with grief, his voice choked. 'Lakshmana, no...'

Meghnada's laughter echoed through the battlefield once more. 'You will never see him rise again, Rama,' as he turned his chariot to return to the Lankan camp, 'Today, you shall lose your brother, and tomorrow you will be dead, too.'

For the first time, a shadow passed over Rama's heart. He had faced countless trials, but seeing Lakshmana lying motionless, wrapped in the dark coils of *Nagapasha*, filled him with dread. His hands trembled, but he fought to steady himself. 'This cannot be,' he whispered, his voice a blend of sorrow and fury.

Vibhishana stepped forward with grave urgency. 'Do not lose hope, Rama,' he said. 'There is still a chance to save him.'

Rama's eyes flickered with a spark of hope. 'How?'

'The great healer Sushena can save Lakshmana,' Vibhishana said, 'but he will need the *Sanjivani* herb from the distant mountains of the Himalayas. It is the only cure for this sorcery.'

Without hesitation, Hanuman, ever Rama's faithful servant, stepped forward. His massive figure seemed to glow with purpose. 'I will go,' he said, his voice filled with determination. 'I will bring back the *Sanjivani*, no matter how far I must travel.'

Rama looked up at his loyal friend. 'Hanuman, you are our only hope. Go swiftly.'

Hanuman bowed, then leapt into the sky, his powerful legs propelling him through the air with the speed of the wind.

Hanuman flew over forests and mountains, his heart burning with urgency. Time was slipping away—he knew Lakshmana's life hung by a thread.

At last, far in the north, Hanuman spotted the majestic mountain Dronagiri. But, he was faced with an overwhelming problem. The mountain was lush with herbs and medicinal plants. The *Sanjivani* herb was indistinguishable among them. Hanuman could not waste time searching for a single herb among thousands. Hanuman lifted the entire peak into the air, and soared back toward the battlefield.

As the first light of dawn broke, Hanuman returned. The Vanaras and Rakshasas alike looked up in awe as Hanuman descended, carrying the massive mountain.

Sushena quickly identified the life-giving *Sanjivani* herb among the plants. He crushed the sacred herb and applied it to Lakshmana's wounds. The herb worked swiftly and Lakshmana's eyes fluttered open.

Rama's heart surged with relief as he embraced his brother. But the time for celebration was brief. In the distance, the battle still raged, and Ravana's forces were far from defeated.

Meghnada, enraged by Lakshmana's survival, returned to the battlefield the next day, his dark sorcery filling the air with a palpable sense of dread. His anger burned hotter than ever.

Lakshmana, his strength restored, stepped forward, his eyes blazing. 'This ends today, Indrajit. No more tricks. No more sorcery. Face me as a warrior.'

With a final surge of power, Lakshmana called upon his divine heritage, invoking an arrow blessed by Indra himself. The arrow, glowing with divine energy, cut through the air. Meghnada's eyes widened in fear as the arrow found its mark, striking him through the chest. His body stiffened, and with a scream of anguish, he was thrown from his chariot, crashing to the ground in a cloud of dust and flame. The mighty Rakshasa prince lay lifeless on the battlefield, his sorcery undone.

Enraged, Ravana donned the *Brahmakavacha,* the impenetrable armour gifted by Brahma, and climbed onto his chariot once more.

'Today, you will taste death, Rama,' Ravana spat, his voice dripping with venom. 'I will wipe you and your miserable army from the face of this earth.'

Rama, standing alongside Lakshmana, merely raised his bow. 'I do not fear you, Ravana. Your cruelty ends here.'

With a cry that shattered the heavens, Ravana unleashed the *Tamasastra,* a weapon of darkness that blotted out the sun. Shadows fell across the battlefield as the demonic energy spread, consuming everything in its path. Thousands of Vanara soldiers dropped to the ground, their cries lost in the roar of Ravana's magic.

Lakshmana moved first, firing arrows that cut through the veil of darkness. 'Stay behind me, brother!' he shouted, charging toward Ravana. But even as he fought valiantly, he could not halt the demon king's advance.

With a snarl, Ravana drew his weapon—another spear, forged in the fires of hell. He hurled it at Lakshmana with all his might, and this time, Lakshmana could not escape. The spear pierced his armour, sending him crashing to the ground once more, blood staining the earth beneath him.

Rama's heart burned with fury. He launched himself at Ravana, their weapons clashing with the force of a hundred storms. Arrows flew like rain, and the very ground cracked beneath their feet. For every strike Ravana delivered, Rama countered with unmatched precision, but the *Brahmakavacha* shielded the demon from harm.

The battle raged until the air itself seemed to scream. In the end, Ravana, bloodied but unbowed, retreated again, unwilling to face the full wrath of Rama just yet.

Once again, both armies fell into a brief lull. In Lanka, Ravana's wrath had ignited a fire in his heart. He gathered his remaining commanders, their faces pale with the thought of facing Rama once more.

'We will strengthen our defences,' Ravana commanded, his voice fierce. 'And we will prepare for a counterattack. I will not let my enemies take my kingdom!'

Meanwhile, Rama and his allies sought counsel from sages, drawing upon ancient wisdom to fortify their strategies. They trained tirelessly, their spirits unyielding. Each Vanara warrior remembered the fallen and fought for their honour.

The battlefield, now a scarred reminder of previous clashes, lay ready for the next confrontation. This time, Indra himself, the king of the heavens, sent a divine chariot to aid Rama. As the sun rose, the tension crackled in the air.

Rama stood upon the golden chariot, his bow gleaming in the fading light. In the distance, Ravana's chariot approached, pulled by monstrous steeds. As they neared each other, the tension in the air grew tangible.

Ravana struck first, unleashing a barrage of fire and lightning, each spell more devastating than the last. Rama parried with arrows that seemed to glow with divine energy, each one countering Ravana's magic. The two chariots circled each other like predators, striking and retreating, neither giving an inch.

At the height of the battle, Ravana aimed for the heart of Indra's chariot. With a mighty strike, he destroyed the flag of the king of the gods. The Vanaras gasped as they watched, the symbol of their divine protection torn asunder.

But Rama was not deterred. He called upon his own power, summoning the *Indrashakti*, a weapon of pure light. As the two powers clashed, the battlefield erupted in blinding brilliance. For a moment, it seemed as though the world itself would be torn apart.

Yet even this was not enough. Ravana, weakened and enraged, was forced to retreat once more. His charioteer, seeing the state of his king, pulled Ravana back, steering the chariot away from the battlefield just before Rama could deliver the killing blow.

Once again, both armies found themselves in a temporary calm. For days, there was no fighting, but the air was thick with anticipation. Troops tended to their wounds, while commanders strategised. Rumours spread like wildfire about Rama's prowess and Ravana's growing desperation.

Ravana, alone in his chamber, looked into a mirror that reflected not only his image but also the dread of impending doom. 'I cannot fail. I will summon all my strength and strike at dawn. This time, I will not relent until the ground runs red with their blood.'

Meanwhile, Rama and Lakshmana strategised, discussing their next move. 'We cannot let him regroup any longer, brother,' Rama urged. 'We must take the fight to him.'

As the sun rose over the horizon, Ravana stepped onto the field, alone and unyielding, his face a mask of determination. The weight of his past decisions hung heavy upon him, yet he bore it like armour. His chariot, adorned with symbols of power, shimmered with dark magic, reflecting the flames of his fury.

'Today, Rama, I shall kill you!' Ravana roared, his voice echoing across the battlefield. The very ground trembled beneath him as he drew his sword, a massive weapon forged in the depths of the inferno, its edge glinting ominously in the light.

Across the field, Rama stood resolute, his golden bow strung tight, an arrow ready to be let loose. 'I will not let your tyranny continue any longer, Ravana. The suffering you have caused ends today!'

With a single nod, the two warriors charged toward each other, their footsteps a thunderous heartbeat of impending doom. The clash of their weapons echoed like the sound of two mountains colliding. Rama's arrows flew like shooting stars, illuminating the darkened sky, while Ravana's sword sliced through the air, countering every strike with ferocious precision.

The battlefield was transformed into a maelstrom of violence and power, each warrior pushing the other to the brink. Rama unleashed divine arrows blessed by the gods, their light piercing through the shadows. Ravana countered with spells that summoned forth storms, dark clouds circling overhead, lightning crackling dangerously close.

'Is this the best you can do, Rama?' Ravana taunted, his voice laced with disdain. 'You are merely a man playing at being a god!'

Rama narrowed his eyes, his determination unwavering. 'And you are a coward hiding behind your magic! Face me as a warrior, Ravana!'

The ground shook as their weapons clashed, a cacophony of chaos erupting with every strike. Ravana fought with the strength of ten thousand demons, each swing of his sword fuelled by centuries of rage and hatred. Yet, Rama matched him blow for blow, his heart fuelled by the love for Sita and the countless souls crushed beneath Ravana's tyranny.

With every exchange, the sky darkened, as nature mourned the devastation wrought by their conflict. The two titans were locked in a deadly dance, each refusing to yield.

The battle lasted six days.

Exhaustion began to creep into their bones. Ravana's breaths came heavier, and his movements slowed. He felt the weight of defeat pressing down upon him, but his pride refused to let him falter.

'Come, Rama! I will show you the depths of my power!' he bellowed, summoning the *Mahapashupatastra,* a weapon so formidable it had once sent the very gods to their knees.

The air crackled with energy, the fabric of reality trembling at the invocation of such power. Rama's heart raced, and he called upon all his strength, gathering the divine energy bestowed upon him.

'Let it be so!' Rama shouted, releasing the *Vishnu Astra.* The two weapons collided in a blinding explosion, illuminating the battlefield in a cataclysmic moment that seemed to stretch into eternity.

As the dust settled, both warriors staggered back, their strength waning. Ravana's body bore the marks of battle—his armour cracked, bloodied, and bruised, but his spirit remained unbroken. 'You think you can defeat me, Rama? I am immortal!' he spat, laughter mixing with his pain.

Night came. Once again, the exhausted warring armies returned to their respective camps to rest.

Eighty-six days had gone past.

TWENTY-FOUR

The Final Farewell

No Turning Back

The moon hung heavily in the night sky, casting a pale glow over the once magnificent city of Lanka. The proud towers and golden domes now seemed like spectres in the dark, their brilliance dulled by the weight of impending destruction. Inside the palace, all were burdened with the knowledge that the end was near. In a private chamber, away from the watchful eyes of courtiers and soldiers, Ravana stood silently by the window, his gaze fixed on the battlefield below. His imposing frame, clad in black armour, was still and rigid, but his mind was a storm of thoughts.

Mandodari entered the room quietly, her steps barely making a sound on the cold marble floor. She had watched her husband transform over the years, from the mighty king she had fallen in love with, to the man who now stood on the precipice of destruction. Her heart ached as she looked at him, knowing that this would be the last night they would ever spend together.

Her voice was soft but filled with sorrow as she spoke, 'My lord, the drums of war grow louder. The final battle approaches, but why must it be so? Why must you go to a war that will only bring death to you and ruin to Lanka?'

Ravana did not turn to face her. His gaze remained fixed in the distance, where the faint flicker of torches from Rama's camp could be seen against the dark ocean that glimmered with soft, reflected moonlight. His voice, though calm, carried the weight of all the decisions he had made, all the sins he had committed.

'It is not the war that brings ruin, Mandodari. It is the fate that the sages had written long before I drew my first breath,' he said, his tone devoid of the anger that once defined him. 'This war is the culmination of a path I set upon long ago. It had been a conscious decision. A decision that I am not allowed to talk about. Suffice to say that, I have played my part in the grand scheme of this creation, as has Kumbhakarna. It is as fate has decreed. A fate written in blood. There is no turning back now.'

Mandodari stepped closer, her eyes welling with unshed tears. She knew her husband too well—his pride, his strength, and his deep sense of destiny. But she also knew the fear he carried, buried deep beneath layers of arrogance and defiance.

'But why, my lord?' she asked, her voice trembling. 'Why must fate be written in blood? Why must pride be your only guide? You have conquered the heavens, defeated the gods, yet now you stand before a battle you cannot win. Is this how it must end?'

Ravana's expression hardened as he finally turned to face her. His dark eyes, once filled with the fire of ambition, now held a sadness that he could not hide from her.

'Do you think I do not know what awaits me?' he said with a wistful smile, his voice quieter now, but no less firm. 'I have foreseen my death, Mandodari. The omens have spoken, and even the heavens have turned their gaze away from me. But I cannot flee from this battle. To run would be to dishonour everything I have built, everything I have fought for.'

Mandodari's heart broke as she heard his words. She knew he was right—there was no turning back. But that didn't stop her from trying to save him, one last time.

'You speak of honour, but what honour is there in dying for a mistake?' she asked, her voice rising in desperation. 'This war, this battle—it was born not of honour, but of an unrighteous act. You seized Sita without reason, and with her, you stole our future. You could have let her go, but your pride would not allow it. And now, you will lose everything.'

Ravana's face darkened at the mention of Sita, and for a moment, his old fury flashed in his eyes. But then, just as quickly, it faded, replaced by a heavy silence. 'Sita remains unsullied. I brought her to Lanka to avenge the dishonour to our clan. Minakshi didn't deserve the terrible punishment meted out to her by the Raghava princes.'

Mandodari bit her lip, stopping herself from responding. Enough had been said on this by the elders to Ravana. The asuras had their rules: eye for an eye. Lakshmana had harmed Minakshi, hence Ravana was justified in abducting Sita according to their rules. Humans lived by a completely different code. They treated their women very differently. Minakshi had demanded that Rama leave his wedded wife Sita and become her lover. Rama refused and directed her to his younger brother Lakshmana, who had scoffed at her, and she had become furious. Her anger was legendary. What happened afterwards was something the Raghava brothers couldn't truly be blamed for. After she returned with her nose chopped off, things had moved at breakneck speed until Ravana had brought Sita to Lanka almost a year ago.

'I have made my choices,' Ravana spoke, cutting through her chain of thought, his voice barely above a whisper. 'And I will bear the consequences.'

Mandodari stepped forward, her hands reaching out to clasp his arm. She could feel the tension in his muscles, the battle raging within him as fiercely as the one waiting outside.

'We have lost our sons, my lord,' she said, her voice breaking. 'Indrajit, Akshay—all of them are gone. Is that not enough suffering for one lifetime? Must I lose you too?'

Ravana's hand clenched into a fist as she spoke of their sons. The loss of Indrajit, his beloved son and heir, was a wound that still bled deep within him. He had seen his sons fall, one by one, on the battlefield, and now, it was his turn. But the weight of their deaths had not broken his resolve—it had only strengthened it.

'My sons died with honour, fighting for their father, for their kingdom,' he said, his voice heavy with grief but unyielding. 'They died as warriors, and I will do the same.'

Mandodari shook her head, tears streaming down her face. 'But what of me?' she whispered, her voice filled with anguish. 'What will become of me when you are gone? I have followed you through every storm, stood by your side through every trial. I have borne the weight of your sins, your ambitions, but this… this is too much. What will I do when I am left all alone?'

Ravana looked down at her, his expression softening for the first time that night. He reached out, brushing a tear from her cheek with a gentleness that seemed out of place in the midst of such darkness.

'You will carry on,' he said softly. 'You have always been stronger than you know, Mandodari. You have been my strength, my anchor, through all of this. When I am gone, you must continue to lead, to protect what remains of our kingdom. Our people will need you.'

Mandodari's heart clenched as she heard his words. She had always known her husband's love, though it was often hidden beneath his pride. But now, as they stood on the brink of the end, she saw the man she had fallen in love with all those years ago.

'But how can I carry on without you?' she asked once again, her voice trembling. 'How can I bear the weight of all that you have left behind?'

Ravana smiled sadly, his hand still resting on her cheek. 'You will find a way. You always have. And when the time comes, you will be remembered not as the wife of Ravana, the conqueror, but as the queen who rebuilt what was lost.'

Mandodari closed her eyes, her tears falling freely now. 'But what of your legacy, my lord? What will become of all that you have built, all that you have fought for?'

Ravana's gaze grew distant as he looked past her,

into the dark night beyond the window. 'My legacy is already written,' he said quietly. 'It is in the hands of fate now, just as it always has been. But you… you must be the one to shape what comes after. Forget my mistakes, Mandodari. Let them fade with me. But remember the good I have done—the kingdom I built, the people I protected.'

Mandodari's voice was barely a whisper as she asked, 'And what of us? What will become of our love?'

Ravana looked down at her, his expression softening once more. 'Our love is beyond the reach of death,' he said, his voice filled with a quiet certainty. 'It will endure, even when I am gone. In this life and the next, you will always carry a part of me with you.'

The wind outside began to howl, and the sound of distant war horns echoed through the night. Ravana knew it was time. He gently pulled away from her, turning toward the door, his armour gleaming in the pale moonlight.

Mandodari watched him go, her heart breaking with each step he took. 'What will I do, my lord?' she called after him, her voice filled with both sorrow and love. 'What will become of me when you are no longer here?'

Ravana paused at the doorway, his back to her, and for a moment, the world seemed to hold its breath. He turned his head slightly, just enough for her to see the outline of his profile in the darkness.

'You will live on, Mandodari,' he said softly. 'And you will honour me by living well. Forget my sins. Remember my love.'

And with those final words, Ravana stepped into the

night, leaving Mandodari standing alone in the shadows of their palace, her heart heavy with the weight of his parting words.

The wind outside carried the distant sound of battle, and as the door slowly closed behind him, Mandodari knew that her life, and the fate of Lanka, would never be the same again.

'Ah, mortals and gods alike, who now gaze upon the fallen Ravana with eyes full of judgement, know this: the line between virtue and sin is a thread spun by destiny, fine as silk and brittle as bone. I, too, have played my part upon this stage, as have you, as have we all. Would you brand me a demon for the path I have trod? Or is it because I have sinned differently from you? What, then, is this measure of righteousness, this fabled notion of good and evil? Are we not all but destiny's pawns, each bound to the role given by fate, each reciting the lines written long before our births?

'I am no stranger to sin, nor do I feign innocence. I have taken what was not mine, defied those who sought to master me, and struck at the gods themselves. But in my defiance, was there not nobility? In my struggle against the chains of the cosmos, was there not greatness? Who among you would bow so easily before a fate so cruelly ordained? I, Ravana, who grasped at immortality not out of greed, but to carve my name upon the canvas of time itself—I have dared. I have reached for the stars, even as the heavens sought to burn me.

'Do not speak to me of righteousness, for righteousness is a shifting wind. What is good to one is a curse to another. To the gods, I am villain; to my people, I am king. To some, I am monster; to others, I am saviour. It is all a matter of the eyes that look upon me, and the role they play in this grand charade. Is Rama, that noble prince, truly more righteous than I? Or is he simply a man born to a different role, playing his part as the hero, while I wear the mask of the foe?

'Ah, the irony! We stand upon this stage, puppets bound by

strings we cannot see, each of us convinced of our own freedom. Yet, even the gods themselves are bound to their parts, Vishnu to his avatars, Shiva to his dance of creation and destruction. And I, Ravana, the Rakshasa King, am yet another actor in this endless play.

'The noble and the ignoble are shadows of the same truth. I have been called arrogant, but tell me, is it arrogance to seek what lies beyond the reach of mortals? Is it not the very essence of greatness to rise beyond the bounds of one's own nature, to strive for divinity, knowing well that the gods themselves will strike you down? What, then, is this so-called righteousness, if not the courage to pursue one's destiny, however doomed it may be?

'Do not weep for me, Lanka, nor pity my fall. I go now not into death, but into another life, into another cycle of birth and death, where the chains of karma will bind me anew. In another age, in another form, I shall rise once more. Perhaps as a prince, perhaps as a demon, but I will always play my part. For that is the way of this world, a wheel turning endlessly, binding us to roles we cannot escape.

'And in the end, what is death but the final act of a play? What is life but a fleeting moment upon the stage, soon forgotten when the curtain falls? I, Ravana, have lived as both king and sinner, as both god and demon. I have seen the heights of the heavens and the depths of despair. And yet, as I stand on the edge of oblivion, I see clearly now that none of it matters. Not good, not evil, not life, not death. We are all but shadows, dancing in the flicker of a flame soon to be extinguished.

'So judge me not by the sins you see, for you too are bound

by the same strings. Play your part, as I have played mine. And when your time comes, you will understand, as I do now, that there is no right and wrong—only the roles we are given, and the choices we make in the moments between.

'I, Ravana, depart not in defeat, but in the knowledge that the wheel of time will turn once more, and I will rise again.'

—Ravana, Emperor of Lanka

TWENTY-FIVE

Wisdom Has No Foe

The Knowledge of Ages

The winds howled, carrying with them the acrid scent of smoke and blood. The skies above were bruised, darkened by the fury of war, and below, the earth was stained by the fallen. The battlefield was a barren wasteland of death and destruction, the air pungent with the smell of charred earth and burning flesh. The once-proud city of Lanka lay shattered, its golden spires crumbling under the weight of the war.

Yet, in the midst of this carnage, a stillness had fallen. Amidst this grim tableau lay Ravana, the once-mighty king of Lanka. His body was broken, yet his pride stood unbowed. Even as death loomed, his spirit flickered fiercely.

Rama stood tall, his bow resting at his side, his eyes heavy with the weight of both triumph and sorrow. His gaze fixed upon the fallen king, knowing that this was not merely the end of a battle but the end of an era. Beside him stood his loyal companions—Lakshmana, Jambavanta, Hanuman, Vibhishana and Angada, with the other Vanaras gathered around; their faces coloured with the relief of a victory that somehow felt hollow.

The war had cost them all dearly.

Rama turned to Lakshmana, who stood with brow furrowed, the weight of war and vengeance still heavy upon his shoulders.

'Lakshmana,' Rama spoke at last, his voice low and measured, yet carrying with it the authority of the ages. 'The moment is at hand, and Ravana's life slips away like the sands of time. Go to him now, before he breathes his last. Though he has been our most bitter enemy, he is also a master of knowledge, a scholar of things vast and deep. Do not let his wisdom perish with him. Ask him to share with you what he knows, for even in his ruin, there is much to be learned.'

Lakshmana, still flushed with the fire of battle, turned to his brother, disbelief flickering across his face. 'To Ravana?' he asked, incredulous. 'He who has caused such suffering? He who has wronged us beyond measure?'

Rama's gaze remained steady, unyielding. 'Indeed, he is our foe, and for his misdeeds, he has paid dearly. But wisdom is not bound by the deeds of men, and even a tyrant may possess the knowledge of ages. Go to him, Lakshmana, not as a conqueror, but as a seeker. There is no shame in learning, even from the fallen.'

For a moment, Lakshmana hesitated, his heart torn between the fury that still burned within him and the obedience he owed his brother. But the will of Rama was law, and so with a heavy sigh, he nodded and turned toward the place where Ravana lay, broken and dying upon the battlefield.

As Lakshmana approached the fallen demon king, the weight of the moment pressed down upon him. Here lay the great Ravana, the once-mighty ruler whose strength had shaken the heavens, now brought low by his own hubris. His body was battered, his breath shallow, yet the fire in his eyes had not yet dimmed.

Lakshmana stood at Ravana's head, his stance rigid, his face set with the grim resolve of duty. 'Ravana,' he began, his voice hard as steel, 'I come not as an enemy, but as one seeking the knowledge that you possess. My brother, Rama, has sent me to hear your wisdom before it is lost to the world. Though you have fallen, your understanding of the universe remains vast. Will you share it, that your legacy might be more than the ruin of war?'

For a long moment, Ravana said nothing, his chest rising and falling in slow, laboured breaths. Lakshmana watched him impatiently. Ravana slowly turned his head to face away from Lakshmana, who scowled and turned to go back to Rama.

'Brother,' Lakshmana said, his voice tight, 'Ravana's arrogance is boundless, even in the face of death. I asked him for the wisdom you sought, and he turned away from me without a word.'

Rama's eyes softened as he looked at his brother. 'Lakshmana, you forget yourself. Ravana is no longer our enemy. His battle is over, and he lies defeated, not just in body, but in soul as well.'

Lakshmana's brow furrowed in confusion. 'I stood by next to him, awaiting his words, to learn what little he might share. Why would he refuse me?'

Rama smiled gently, his hand resting on Lakshmana's shoulder. 'It is because you stood by his head. When you seek knowledge, you must approach with humility, as a student approaches a master. Go to Ravana's feet, for even in death, there is honour.'

Lakshmana, taken aback by his brother's gentle rebuke, bowed his head and walked back, still burning with pride. This time he kneeled at Ravana's feet, where the dust of the earth mingled with the blood of the fallen. His heart slowly gave way to respect, and his voice softened as he spoke again.

'Ravana, mighty King of Lanka,' Lakshmana said, 'I come to you not as a victor, but as a student, seeking the knowledge that you, in your many years, have gathered. Share with me, not for my sake, but for the sake of this world.'

A faint smile, touched with bitterness and regret, curled on Ravana's lips. 'Ah, Lakshmana… Now you speak as one who seeks wisdom, not glory.'

The silence of the battlefield deepened, as Ravana, now at the edge of death, gathered the last remnants of his strength. His eyes, though clouded with the shadow of mortality, gleamed with the fire of a mind that had known the breadth of the universe. His voice, once like thunder that shook the heavens, now came as a low murmur, yet it held the weight of the cosmos.

'Hear me well, Lakshmana,' Ravana began, his words deliberate, each one carrying the gravity of his final moments. 'For I have learned much, and in what little time I have left, I shall give you the wisdom that remains within me.'

He paused, drawing in a laboured breath, the rasp of death close, but his words sharp as ever. 'First… do not make enemies of those closest to you—the ones who stand by your side every day, the ones whose hands deliver your food, whose words open doors for you, whose strength drives your chariot. Even your brother... should not be your enemy. They hold your life in their hands, Lakshmana, in ways you cannot see. They can destroy you from within.'

Lakshmana felt a shiver pass through him, for though he had never thought of such things, the truth of Ravana's words struck deep.

'Next,' Ravana continued, his breath growing more strained, 'never think you are invincible, even if victory follows you like a shadow. I thought myself beyond defeat, beyond the reach of men or gods. But even the greatest fall, Lakshmana. Even kings bleed, and I… I have bled.'

Ravana's chest heaved with the effort of speech, but he pushed on, driven by a need to impart what had been learned through the bitterness of his long life. 'Beware of those who speak sweetly, who flatter you with words of praise. They are the true poison, the ones who seek to blind you with their honeyed lies. Instead, trust the voice of dissent, the one who dares to criticise you, who speaks with harsh truth. It is they who will guide you rightly, even when their words burn.'

Lakshmana became contemplative as Ravana's wisdom took root in his mind. The battlefield around them seemed to fade, as the dying king's words filled the air with their power.

'Never… never underestimate your enemy,' Ravana said, his voice now a mere whisper. 'I thought Hanuman was nothing more than a monkey. I dismissed him as a nuisance. And yet, he burned my city, he humbled my armies. My arrogance blinded me to his strength, as it did with you and your brother. Never forget, Lakshmana, that even the smallest of enemies can bring about your ruin if you are not careful.'

Lakshmana, deep in thought, bowed his head low, the weight of Ravana's lessons pressing heavily on him.

'Lastly…' Ravana breathed, his life slipping away with each word, 'know this, Lakshmana. You cannot escape fate. The stars… they weave the threads of our lives, and though you may fight, though you may struggle, they will bring you what is destined. I thought I could outwit the gods themselves, that I could bend the universe to my will… but in the end, the stars pulled me to this moment, this end.'

The wind, which had been still, seemed to stir softly around them, carrying Ravana's final words like a whisper through the field.

'And Lakshmana… whether you love the gods, or hate them… do so with all your heart. Let your devotion, or your hatred, be fierce and unrelenting. For the gods… they respond to those who feel deeply, who burn with passion. I hated them, but they knew my name… because I hated them well.'

Lakshmana raised his head slowly, his eyes meeting Ravana's, and in that moment, he saw not a demon, but a king—a king who had loved fiercely, who had fought fiercely, who had lived and was now dying by the strength of his convictions, flawed though they were.

A moment of silence passed, and Lakshmana felt a frisson rise up his spine, not from the cool air, but from the truth of Ravana's words—the cold, inevitable truth of fate.

Ravana's eyes began to close, as his chest rose and fell weakly. The fire that had once burned so fiercely within him was now no more than a faint ember, but Lakshmana, in that moment, saw the greatness that had once defined this king. It was not the greatness of his conquests, nor his strength in battle, but the greatness of one who had lived with fierce conviction, even if that conviction had led to his downfall.

Lakshmana bowed low, his forehead touching the ground in a gesture of respect. 'Thank you, O Ravana, King of Lanka,' he said softly, his voice filled with a newfound humility. 'Your wisdom will not die with you.'

Ravana's hand stirred faintly at his side, as if to acknowledge Lakshmana. Without another word, Lakshmana rose to his feet and turned away. His heart was heavy, not with triumph, but with the knowledge that even the greatest of enemies could be more than they seemed. The battlefield seemed distant now, as though it belonged to another world. He walked slowly back to where Rama stood, his mind filled with the weight of Ravana's final teachings.

Rama did not speak, but his eyes were soft with understanding. He knew what had passed between Lakshmana and Ravana, and there was no need for further words. Lakshmana took his place beside his brother, his heart filled with the strange, bittersweet knowledge that the wisdom of a king, even one as dark as Ravana, could shine brighter than any victory.

TWENTY-SIX

The Rakshasa Who Would Be King

Twilight of the Mighty

The battlefield of Lanka lay silent under a dimming sky, the sun bleeding into the horizon, casting long shadows over the fallen. Smoke rose from distant fires, curling like ghostly hands in the air. The earth, once resplendent with the gold and splendour of Lanka's glory, was now dark and torn, littered with the bodies of warriors who had fought till their last breath for the ambitions of their king.

And there, amidst the devastation, lay Ravana, the king of kings, the conqueror of the heavens and the earth. His once-invincible form, clad in armour now cracked and bloodied, sprawled upon the ground like a fallen titan. The wound at his navel, where Rama's arrow had struck, still smouldered, a thin line of blood trickling from it. But his life force had not yet faded. His chest still rose with shallow, laboured breaths, and his gaze was sharp as it scanned the darkening sky.

'How cruelly does fate play its hand,' he thought. 'The wheel of time turns, and the great are brought low, not by the strength of their enemies, but by the workings of destiny.'

He had known this day would come. Long before Rama's army had marched upon his golden city, Ravana had seen it. It was not Rama's strength nor his divine bow that had felled him, but a force older, more inevitable. Fate. He had pushed forward regardless, knowing that resistance was futile. For what is a king if he does not defy even the gods themselves?

Now, he lay at the feet of the very destiny he had sought to outwit. But even in this, there were truths hidden from those who thought they knew him, and those who thought they had defeated him.

The sound of footsteps pulled Ravana from his thoughts. He shifted his gaze and saw Vibhishana approaching. His brother, who had betrayed him, whose face now appeared twisted with sorrow. Ravana could almost laugh at the irony. Here was the brother who had stood against him in battle, but now, as the war's tide receded, it was not triumph that filled Vibhishana's heart, but grief.

'Even victory brings no joy when it comes at the cost of blood,' Ravana mused. 'Dharma, the great and noble ideal, is nothing but a chain that binds men. Those who believe themselves righteous are often blind to the hand that truly guides their actions.'

Vibhishana knelt beside him, his face pale, his voice heavy with unspoken guilt. Ravana's lips curled into a faint, bitter smile. 'You come to seek forgiveness now, after all that has transpired?'

Vibhishana bowed his head low, the burden of his choice weighing on his every word. 'I followed the path of dharma, but my heart has known no peace since. I acted as I believed I must, but it has cost me my brother—my blood. I am not here to seek forgiveness, but to ask how I can ease the pain of your passing.'

Ravana's gaze bore into his brother. 'You speak of dharma, yet what is dharma but the will of those above us, those who have set the world in motion? You, who once stood beside me, now choose to stand with the enemy, believing that righteousness has chosen you. But righteousness is a fleeting shadow, Vibhishana. It is the victor's truth. The gods use us all in their games, and you are no more than a pawn in this tale.'

The air between them grew still, heavy with the weight of unsaid words. Ravana lay all alone now, abandoned by the very world he had sought to rule. And yet, even in defeat, there was no regret in his heart. Regret was for the weak, for those who sought the approval of others. Ravana had never needed anyone's approval but his own.

'Do you think I fear death?' Ravana asked quietly, his gaze drifting toward the blood-red sky. 'Do you think this wound, this mortal blow, is what shakes me?'

Vibhishana dared not raise his eyes. 'Great one, your fall grieves me. I wish only to honour you, to ensure your name is not lost to history.'

Ravana's laugh was low and bitter, like the last rumble of a dying storm. 'History will remember me, have no doubt about that. Not as you wish, but as I have chosen. A king does not fear death, Vibhishana. To die is nothing. It is obscurity that is the true death. But I will not be forgotten. As long as men whisper my name, as long as my story is told, I shall live on. That is true immortality.

You may kill my body, but my legacy will live long after your dharma fades to dust.'

The sun had nearly disappeared beneath the horizon, leaving the battlefield cloaked in twilight. In the distance, Rama stood with his bow lowered, watching, but he did not intervene. This moment belonged to Ravana and his brother.

'Great one,' Vibhishana began again, his voice shaking, 'I did not seek this outcome. My heart is burdened with sorrow, for you were the mightiest among us. There was none like you in all the worlds.'

Ravana's eyes flickered, the fire in them dimming for a moment. 'There never will be. You have betrayed me, but I hold no hatred in my heart for you. It was written long ago that you would stand against me. You are merely an instrument, just as I am. Fate is not something you or I can escape. But know this: your righteousness, your dharma, is as much a trap as the sins you despise in me.'

Vibhishana looked up, startled. 'But you, great one, are the king of Lanka, the conqueror of the heavens. How could you—'

'Dharma is not the end, Vibhishana. It is the means by which we justify our actions to ourselves. But it is no more real than the illusions we craft in our minds. What you see as righteousness, I see as the shackles of fate. I have seen beyond this world, and I know that we are bound by forces far beyond our understanding.'

Ravana's gaze shifted toward Rama, who stood like a figure carved from stone, unaware of the deeper truth behind his own actions. Rama, the prince of Ayodhya and warrior of virtue, was none other than Vishnu incarnate—

the god who had once granted Ravana his boons, now come to undo the very life he had empowered. Yet, Rama himself did not fully comprehend the depth of this cosmic play.

Ravana had known the truth from the moment he laid eyes on Rama. Long ago, in a previous incarnation, he and his brother Vijaya had stood as gatekeepers at Vaikuntha, barring entry to the four Kumaras, the ancient sages who had cursed them both. They were destined to be reborn as the enemies of the very god they served. Thus, Ravana had played this role twice already, meeting his end at the hands of Vishnu's incarnations, as fate had demanded. It was a curse that bound them both—a cosmic dance of destruction and rebirth, where Ravana was cast both as villain and devotee.

'He does not know,' Ravana thought with a faint smile. In a faint whisper, he spoke almost to himself, 'Not yet. Even Vishnu, in this mortal form, is blind to the full measure of what binds us to each other. He believes he has come here to end my reign, but there is a far deeper reason—a reason neither he nor any of the gods can comprehend.'

Vibhishana's brow furrowed as he caught some of the words. 'What are you saying, great one? What is it you know that I cannot see?'

Ravana's voice lowered further, his words carrying the weight of untold eons. 'You will not understand, brother. There are some truths too vast for the mortal mind to hold. It is Rama's arrow that brings me to the threshold of death. It is a dance we have been fated to perform, life after life. Rama, just like you, sees only a righteous battle, a struggle of good and evil. But it is more than that—it has always been more than that.'

The cryptic nature of Ravana's words unsettled Vibhishana. His brother had always been a mystery, a man whose mind was a labyrinth of ambition, wisdom, and madness. Even now, as he lay wounded on the battlefield, he spoke not with the clarity of a man at death's door, but with the foresight of one who had peered beyond the veil of mortal understanding.

Vibhishana lowered his head again. 'Then what is to come, great one? If this is all fate, what awaits us now?'

Ravana's breath came slower, but his voice remained strong. 'You will live, Vibhishana. You will rule Lanka, and you will bring it peace. That is your destiny. But know this—ruling is not the same as conquering. You will learn what it means to lead a people who once called me their king.'

Vibhishana's eyes filled with tears. 'I will honour your memory, great one. I will lead as best I can.'

Ravana's gaze softened, a strange sadness filled the space between them. 'Honour is not enough, dear brother. You must learn from my mistakes. You must wield power with compassion, understanding that a ruler's strength lies not in fear, but in love for his people.'

The twilight deepened, and stars began to twinkle faintly. The universe itself bore witness to this profound exchange. Ravana shifted slightly, grimacing as pain flared from his wound, yet his voice held firm, echoing with the wisdom of the ages.

'Remember, Vibhishana, pride is a fleeting shadow that can eclipse even the brightest of minds. Do not let the allure of power blind you to the needs of your subjects. If you truly wish to honour me, it must be through the legacy of a compassionate ruler.'

Ravana closed his eyes for a moment before continuing, 'Mandodari is the heart of this kingdom. She deserves better than to be cast aside in my absence. You will take care of her, Vibhishana. You must protect her and provide for her. A woman of her strength and spirit should not have to grieve alone. She will need you by her side. You have always stood for what is right, even when that path led you away from me. You will win her trust. You must, for she is a part of my legacy, a thread woven into the fabric of my story. Protect her, and you will keep a part of me alive in this world.'

Vibhishana nodded, understanding the depth of his brother's request. 'I will not fail you.'

As the darkness began to envelop the land, Ravana felt a calm wash over him. His eyes turned to the stars that flickered above, vast and indifferent, yet so deeply intertwined with their fates. 'Embrace the knowledge gained from those who came before you. There is strength in humility, and in recognising the limits of our power. The universe is filled with mysteries, Vibhishana. Even gods are nothing but players in a grand cosmic drama. In your heart, you must carry the knowledge that each life is but a chapter in an eternal book. Your time will come, and you must not squander it.'

'What do you mean, great one?' Vibhishana asked, bewildered by his brother's enigmatic words.

'Life is cyclical, a great wheel that spins onward. We are bound to these cycles, destined to meet and part, to learn and to forget. My passing will set off a chain of events that will echo through the ages, shaping the future in ways we cannot yet fathom. I have embraced my fate. Death is but another journey, and I shall walk it with the dignity befitting a king. What lies beyond is not for us to know, only to accept.'

Ravana's breath grew shallow, each inhale a struggle, yet his spirit burned brightly. 'Do not grieve for me, Vibhishana. Remember, the greatest strength lies in understanding oneself.'

The darkened sky overhead whispered secrets of ages past, and Ravana felt a profound sense of closure. His life, filled with ambition and pride, had led him to this moment, but it would not end here. The cycle would continue, a dance of life and death, as eternal as the stars.

'Embrace the trials ahead, dear brother,' Ravana said, his voice now barely a whisper. 'In every challenge, there is an opportunity for growth. Remember my words, and you will carry my spirit with you, into the hearts of our people. Lead them well, and perhaps one day, you will understand the grand design that weaves us together across lifetimes.'

With those final words, Ravana's eyes began to close. His breathing grew more laboured, but there was no fear in his heart. He felt a release, a weight lifting as he surrendered to the inevitable. He had lived fiercely, loved deeply, and fought bravely. As darkness crept into his vision, he found solace in the knowledge that his legacy would endure, transformed through Vibhishana's hands.

'Goodbye, dear brother,' he managed to say, his voice a mere whisper. 'You will find your way.'

Rama stood watching the exchange from afar. Somehow, he was filled with a mixture of sadness and relief, as the once-mighty king of Lanka drifted into eternal slumber.

Epilogue

Vaikuntha Regained

'Mortals, heed the fall of Ravana, for in my downfall lies the lesson of humility, the path to redemption, and the eternal truth of the universe. In my end, see the consequences of unbridled ambition and the ultimate wisdom of humility. May my three lives, struggles, and deaths in this mortal plane, serve as beacons guiding all who seek power and wisdom, and remind you that true greatness lies not in conquest, but in understanding and harmony with the divine order.

'Reflect upon my words, for they are a warning: ambition unchecked and pride untempered lead to ruin. The cycle of life and death is a relentless teacher. My story is not one of mere defeat, but of the eternal struggle for redemption through trials of one's own making. Remember me not only for my power but for my folly. Let my tale be a lesson: true strength lies not in defiance of the divine, but in understanding and accepting one's place in the cosmos. As my life force drains, I relinquish my pride and embrace the peace that has eluded me for lifetimes. I see the futility of my defiance, the hollowness of my conquests.'

With his final breath, Ravana's voice carried across the battlefield, leaving behind a legacy of might and a warning to all who dare to challenge the divine.

Acknowledgements

I offer my heartfelt gratitude to everyone who has supported me in bringing *Ravana: Destiny's Cursed* to life.

I remain deeply indebted to the scholars, storytellers, and guardians of India's ancient epics and mythological traditions. Their lifelong commitment to understanding the many layers of Ravana's legacy has both guided and inspired my own journey through his tale.

I am especially thankful to Vikas Rakheja of Amaryllis for his steadfast support and perceptive guidance, and to my editor, Bidisha Srivastava, whose thoughtful insights and meticulous care have shaped this narrative with great sensitivity and depth. I am grateful to Trinankur Banerjee for his fabulous cover art, which has captured the essence of Ravana's inner conflict with remarkable depth and beauty.

To my readers—thank you for walking with me into the shadowed, complex, and haunting world of Ravana. Your curiosity and engagement give purpose to this endeavour.